Enoch Edwin Byrum

Divine Healing of Soul and Body

Enoch Edwin Byrum

Divine Healing of Soul and Body

ISBN/EAN: 9783337779221

Printed in Europe, USA, Canada, Australia, Japan

Cover: Foto ©Lupo / pixelio.de

More available books at **www.hansebooks.com**

Divine Healing

OF

Soul and Body.

ALSO

HOW GOD HEALS THE SICK, AND THE CONDITIONS UPON WHICH THEY ARE RESTORED; GIVING WONDERFUL TESTIMONIES OF HIS MIRACULOUS POWER IN THESE LAST DAYS.

By E. E. BYRUM.

GRAND JUNCTION MICH.:
GOSPEL TRUMPET PUBLISHING CO,
1892,

AUTHOR'S PREFACE.

In sending forth this volume for the benefit of suffering humanity, it is hoped that many who are bound down by sin and sickness, and oppressed of the devil, will be enabled to better understand the will of God concerning themselves; and by a closer walk with him, can by faith unlock the rich treasure house of the Lord, and enjoy the blessings of his love as never before.

Many volumes have been written on the subject of Divine Healing, yet most people—even professing Christians all over the land—are skeptics regarding the same, because they have been taught from their youth up that "the day of miracles is past." Such has been taught at home, from the press and the pulpit; inasmuch as to say that the Lord's power is limited; making Him a finite being, instead of infinite

It is the aim of this work to show forth the principles of salvation, and how to reach the highest attainments; and encourage people to believe the Word of God, and not fear to walk out upon His promises. As the subject treated upon is one against which there is much prejudice, I trust no one will lay the book aside until the whole of it is read and compared with the sacred Word.

God forbid that any one whose name is mentioned in this book should receive self-praise or glory for the works wrought through them by the power of God; but may He only be adored, who is worthy of all honor and praise. May the Lord bless the dear ones who have so kindly aided in this work by sending in their testimonies; also a dear brother who kindly contributed the chapter on "The Use of Divine Healing." For want of space we have had to omit many precious and wonderful testimonies which were sent in for publication.

That our heavenly Father will bless each reader of this book, with a fervent trust in Him, and enable them to enjoy the blessing of health, and full salvation, is the earnest prayer of your humble servant.

Yours in Him.

E. E. BYRUM.

Grand Junction, Mich., *April 7, 1892.*

CONTENTS.

Part I.—Divine Healing of The Soul.

	Page.
The Darkness of Sin	9
The Way Out	10
The Sinner's Call	11
Conviction	13
Consecration	15
Faith	17
Conversion	23
Sanctification	26
The Two Works of Grace	34

Part II.—Divine Healing of The Body.

The Doctrine of Healing	49
Is The Day of Healing Past?	53
The Use of Divine Healing	59
Old Testament Witnesses	67
New Testament Witnesses	76
The Apostasy	87
The Evening Light	95
The Promise of His Power	99
The Gifts of Healing	100
Who Are The Elders?	105
What Kind of Oil to Use	107
Anointing and Consecration	107
Can I Be Healed?	109
Sick For The Glory of God	109
The Use of Medicine	112

Means Which God Blesses . 113
The Prayer of Faith 116
Walking Out Upon His Promises 118
Resisting Temptation 121
Resisting The Truth 122
Hindrances to Healing . 123
Casting Out Devils 124
Sending Anointed Handkerchiefs . 126
Spiritualism 128
Christian Science 130
Witnesses Since The Apostles . . 131

PART III.—WITNESSES OF TO DAY.

A Wonderful Deliverance . 135
The Blind Eyes Opened 142
Nine Years an Invalid . . . 145
Corroborating Testimony . . 149
Physicians Baffled for Eleven Years . . 151
Deliverance from Disobedience . . 152
Healed, Soul, Body and Eyes . . 155
Motherhood 157
He Healeth Our Diseases . . . 163
Touched with Divine Power . . 165
A Trial of Faith 170
Marvelous Healing of The Soul 175
The Family Physician 182
Healed of Rheumatism and a Stiff Joint . 183
A Crushed Arm Healed 187
Healed of Tumor . . 189
At Death's Door . . 190
Heart Disease Cured . . 191
Healed of Catarrh . . . 192
Healed of Cancer . . . 194
Restoration of Eyesight . . 196

CONTENTS.

Nasal Catarrh Instantly Healed	197
A Wonderful Cure of Consumption	199
A Little Boy's Prayer Answered	202
How God Delivered Me	206
A Warning Against Opium	217
Devils Cast Out	219
The Blind and Lame See and Walk	221
Broken Bone Healed	223
An Anointed Handkerchief Applied	224
The Chastening Rod	226
A Friend in Affliction	230
Crutches Thrown Away	233
Healing of Cancer and Consumption	235
The Lord is My Physician	238
A Wonderful Answer to Prayer	239
A Change of Physicians	241
Confirming Testimony	242

DIVINE HEALING OF THE SOUL.

PART 1.
CHAPTER I.
THE DARKNESS OF SIN.

In reading the sacred Word, we find that God has made provision for the healing of both soul and body. The Psalmist says it is the Lord "who forgiveth all thine iniquities; who healeth all thy diseases."—Psa. 103: 3.

When man was first placed here on earth he was on a plane with God; was in a holy state, without sin or sickness; but through his disobedience "sin entered into the world, and death by sin; and so death passed upon all men, for that all have sinned."—Rom. 5: 12. This death was a spiritual one, and was the result of the seed of sin which the enemy of souls planted in them causing them to be driven from the garden of Eden.

Adam was born in the likeness of God, but after his fall by sin he begat children in his own likeness, after his own image. Thus all persons thereafter, inherited this evil nature; and as soon as they reach the age of accountability, and know the difference between good and evil, they become transgressors. Although innocent at birth, but few years pass by until this inherited nature leads them into the ways of sin: and the "wages of sin is death."

The person who is traveling the way of sin, and rapidly going the downward road to ruin without a ray of heavenly light, indeed has a sin-sick soul, which only the great Physician can heal.

CHAPTER II.
THE WAY OUT.

Through all this spiritual darkness there is but one way out, and that is by the way of the cross. It is through the blood of Jesus Christ, which was shed upon the cross of Calvary, that the atonement was made for our sins. "For God so loved the world that he gave his only begotten Son, that whosoever believeth in him should not perish, but have everlasting life."—Jno. 3: 16.

The prophets of old foretold the coming of this great Redeemer who would redeem the people from their sins. Yea, even the angel of the Lord, told Joseph that his wife should bring forth a son, and said: "Thou shalt call his name JESUS: and he shall save his people from their sins." His life was a sinless one, yet he was reviled and persecuted on every hand, and even suffered the agonies of death upon the cross, that poor vile sinners might have eternal life, and an everlasting inheritance with him in glory. He says, "I am the way, the truth, and the life."

We are to take Christ for our example, "who did no sin, neither was guile found in his mouth: who when he was reviled, reviled not again; when he suffered, he threatened not; but committed himself to him that judgeth righteously: who his own self bare our sins in his own body on the tree, that we, being dead to sins, should live unto righteousness: by whose stripes ye were healed."—1 Peter 2: 22–24.

CHAPTER III.
THE SINNER'S CALL.

The Bible teaches us that there is a future home prepared for all mankind where they will dwell throughout eternity. For the wicked, it is a place of endless torment in hell, from whence there is no returning; no future redemption beyond the grave. For the righteous, there is a home of everlasting peace and joy in heaven where they will forever praise God in glory.

We have a gracious God, one whose mercies can not be fathomed; they are boundless, and are extended unto all. We are free moral agents, that is,— it is our privilege to choose Christ as our Savior, or reject him, and whatever the decision may be, our choice is either heaven or hell. It is not the will of the Father that any one should perish, and he commands all men everywhere to repent.

Dear reader, are you burdened with sin, and your life made miserable on account of the lost condition of your soul? Remember that Jesus is the door into the kingdom and he is still calling: "Come unto me, all ye that labor and are heavy laden, and I will give you rest. Take my yoke upon you and learn of me: for I am meek and lowly in heart: and ye shall find rest unto your souls: for my yoke is easy, and my burden is light."—Matt. 11: 28-30.

"Ho, every one that thirsteth, come ye to the waters, and he that hath no money; come ye, buy and eat; yea, come, buy wine and milk without money and without price. Wherefore do ye spend money for that which is not bread? and your labor for that which satisfieth not? Hearken diligently unto me, and eat ye that which is good, and let your soul delight itself in fatness."

"Seek ye the Lord while he may be found, call ye upon him while he is near.

"Let the wicked forsake his way, and the unrighteous man his thoughts, and let him return unto the Lord, and he will have mercy upon him; and to our God, for he will abundantly pardon."–Isa. 55: 1, 2, 6, 7.

"Though your sins be as scarlet, they shall be white as snow; though they be red like crimson, they shall be as wool."—Isa. 1: 18.

"Whosoever will may come." O what precious promises! No one is excluded if they will obey the call and do His commands." Seek and ye shall find." "Knock and it shall be opened unto you."

The sinner hears these words of the Lord spoken, and the gentle calls bring conviction upon his soul.

CHAPTER IV.
CONVICTION.

As the sinner begins to realize his condition before God, eternity stares him in the face, and sin weighs heavy upon his soul. The darkness increases and the burden becomes greater until life is miserable. O what a condition! lost! forever lost unless God extends his mercy and offers deliverance to the captive soul. The sentence has gone forth from the mouth of the Lord, " Except ye repent ye shall all likewise perish." Yet many harden their hearts, and go on heedless and apparently unconcerned, but that does not change the sentence in the least. When any one is arraigned before the courts of justice for some crime or misdemeanor, and is tried according to the laws of the land and found guilty, then the supreme judge passes the sentence of punishment. It then makes no difference whether that person feels that he will be punished or not, the punishment will be carried out just the same. Just so with the sinner who has transgressed the law of God, and disobeyed his holy word: God calls upon him to repent and make restitution. And the refusal of the same, and utter rejection of the commands and laws of the Lord will bring his judgments upon such a person. And when life on earth shall pass away, eternity will reveal the awful fact that the penalty is to be carried out, and the wrath of a just God will forever be upon a doomed soul.

Conviction is not feeling, as many suppose, but conviction of sin generally brings on a feeling of remorse. It is then when mercy reaches forth a helping hand of deliverance, but to reject the proffered help is to drive away the gentle Spirit which inclined the soul to turn to God, and a continual rejection may so harden the heart as to drive away the feeling of remorse; but the case has already been tried before the great tribunal of God and the decision rendered, GUILTY. The doom is eternal punishment unless repentance is made before life closes the mortal scene. There is still hope for those who will yet turn unto the Lord.

A knowledge of the condition of the soul is sufficient, without a worked-up feeling about the matter. But it takes something more to set the heart right than merely being convicted of sin. It requires a genuine consecration, and submission of all things unto God and a willingness to forsake sin and do his will.

CHAPTER V.
CONSECRATION.

We would not picture the horrors of hell, nor present the awful doom of sinners and urge them unto repentance, could we not point them to a better place; one prepared only for the redeemed to dwell with Christ in glory. That place is heaven. A place where no sorrow can enter; and the blood-washed throng enter the joys of the Lord to go no more out forevermore. Such a place is worth gaining at the cost of all things, and it takes an unconditional surrender to God in order to be fitted for entrance. This life is the dressing room for the future. We must have on the wedding garment and be ready with our lamps trimmed and burning when the Bridegroom comes, otherwise we will be like the five foolish virgins, forever shut out. The soul now begins to earnestly cry out for mercy, saying, " What shall I do to be saved?" The inspired

Word answers, Repent of your sins. Acts 17: 30.

"Repent ye therefore and be converted, that your sins may be blotted out."—Acts 3: 19.

"Except ye repent ye shall all likewise perish."—Luke 13: 3, 5.

FIRST, Forsake your sins. Isa. 55: 7.

SECOND, Confess your sins. Prov. 28: 13.

"If we confess our sins he is faithful and just to forgive us our sins."—1 Jno. 1: 9.

"Believe on the Lord Jesus Christ and thou shalt be saved."—Acts 16: 31; Jno. 3: 16, 18.

To make the necessary consecration to bring the soul out of the darkness of sin into the light of heaven, requires something more than going through a mere form. It takes a yielding to the will of God; a determination to forsake all sin and follow Jesus; an action in response to his commands.

When persons have done what the Lord requires of them, they will find the Lord true to his promise. He says if you confess your sins he will forgive: if you believe on the Lord Jesus Christ you shall be saved; and many other precious promises are given. To acknowledge your sins and then continue doing the same as before would not be Bible confession, neither would God accept such, for the evil man is commanded to forsake his ways. The moment the consecration is complete, the Lord answers prayer by doing the work. But there are too many like Ananias and Sapphira, who try to keep back a part of the price, and hide it away for future use for themselves; are unwilling to make a complete surrender, just as if they could hide something from the all-searching eye of God, who seeth all things, and knoweth the most secret thoughts. He knows when a consecration is a sham and when it is genuine, and his contracts always stand filled and signed, ready to pass at full value as soon as the conditions are met on our part.

CHAPTER VI.
FAITH.

Faith in God is taking him at his word, and moving out upon his promises with all confidence and sincerity without a doubt or fear. It is the "substance of things hoped for, the evidence of things not seen." "But without faith it is impossible to please him; for he that cometh to God must believe that he is, and that he is a rewarder of them that diligently seek him."—Heb. 11: 1, 6.

How often people come to a point of consecration where they say they have done all the Word of God requires of them, and yet cannot claim the blessing of God! What is the trouble? If the consecration is complete the promises of the Word can be claimed without a doubt, whether a person has any outward evidence or not. If we believe God, why hesitate to count his promises true and claim them as our own? There is a lesson which every one must learn who are seeking blessings from the treasure house of the Lord, and that is to believe they do receive that for which they ask; and that God does hear now and answer the request the very moment the conditions of his word are met. Remember the Savior said: "What things soever ye desire, when ye pray, believe that ye receive them and ye shall have them."–Mark 11: 24. These promises are to his children; those who walk not after the things of this world, but have forsaken all things that would bind them to the sinful pleasures of life. They are for any one who will forsake sin and obey God.

Genuine faith in God is something more than moving out upon his promises no further than we can see with our natural eyes, and believing only as far as we can see, and as providence performs in our sight. It means a decisive action of belief against all opposing elements and mountains of adversities that may seemingly bar the way to prevent an answer to prayer. The one who prays the prayer of faith calls upon God for the desired favor and leaves the result with him, knowing that according to his word it shall come to pass.

Too many get the wrong idea regarding the nature of faith, and imagine it is for almost anyone else but themselves; that in order to exercise faith they must wonderfully and rigorously exercise the mind, and strain and worry, or go through certain performances in order to grasp the promise and secure His blessings. There are just two platforms upon which to stand, and we must take one or the other. The one is BELIEF, the other UNBELIEF. The Word of God is true, or it is not true. He will do as he has promised, or he will not do it. His promises are reliable, or they are not reliable. Then the question is, Will we consider the Word of God true, or shall we believe it to be false? If we consider him to be a true God, why hesitate to obey and move out upon his promises, whether we can see our way through or not, on account of the adversities and many opposing elements with which we may have to contend? When we are in the order of the Lord and desire a favor of him, it is evidence enough to know he has promised in his word; and, if so, we need not seek after signs and wonders in order to verify his promises, or give evidence that he will not fail to fulfill his promises.

To one seeking a favor of God the point of faith or trust must be reached in which the action of present belief takes place; a positive confidence that he hears and answers just now, for, "This is the confidence that we have in him, that if we ask anything according to his will he heareth us; and if we know that he hear us, whatsoever we ask, we know that we have the petitions that we desired of him."—1 Jno. 5: 14, 15. "And whatsoever ye shall ask in my name, that will I do, that the Father may be glorified in the Son. If ye shall ask anything in my name I will do it."—Jno 14: 13, 14.

The SINNER must believe that NOW is the accepted time, NOW is the day of salvation.—1 Cor. 6:2. And, "If we confess our sins he is faithful and just to forgive us our sins."—1 Jno. 1: 9.

The BELIEVER must realize these words as true, demanding immediate attention: "This is the will of God even your sanctification."—1 Thess. 4:3. "Go on to perfection."—Heb. 6: 1. The Father will give you another Comforter.—Jno. 14:16. "Present your bodies a living sacrifice, holy, acceptable unto God, which is your reasonable service."—Rom. 12: 1.

The AFFLICTED must remember that "the prayer of faith shall save the sick, and the Lord will raise him up."—Jas. 5: 13–15.

It is generally our own choice if we are bound down, either by sin or the discouragements of life. God promises to break the fetters and set the captive free. Although one may be bound with chains of iron and steel, yet that cannot deprive perfect freedom and joy in the soul.

Suppose a man were bound down hand and foot and cast into prison, and would make an appeal for pardon, and the jailor would come and present the papers showing that his request had been granted by the authorities, would he not begin to feel grateful toward those who had granted the pardon? But the jailor reads the pardon, takes off the fetters and chains, takes down the prison bars, throws open the door and says, "You are now a free man: go your way in peace." But the man still sits there and says: "I know the pardon reads that I am to be free, and I believe every word of it, but I am yet in prison."

"The doors are open, come out," says the jailor.

"I know they are open, and I know I would be free if I were out, but I am not out."

"Well, come out," still insists the jailor; "do you not believe what I have said and done is all true?"

"O yes, I believe every word of it, but it seems as if I never will get out of here."

A pardon would be of no benefit to such a man, because of his own choice he remains in prison and does not act upon the privileges given. That is faith without works. Yet how often we see persons seeking salvation who are in just such a condition. They believe, and yet in a sense they do not believe. They seem to be afraid that God will not do what he has said he will do. Is that not worse than doubting

Thomas? Our Bible teaches us that faith and works go together. While it is not necessary to wait for a certain amount of feeling in order to exercise faith, yet when our faith is exercised according to his word, it will leave its effect; the thing believed for will be received whether it comes in just the way we are expecting it or not. Often people ask God for something, and do not get it because they will not receive it in the way in which he offers it to them. For instance, a man is seeking the pardon of his sins, and has made up his mind he must have an experience the moment he complies with the Word, such as will cause him to leap and bound and shout the high praises of God; and because he has seen these manifestations in others at the time of pardon, thinks he must have the same manifestations to witness the work done, and thus measure salvation from a standpoint of feeling instead of faith, and is very apt to receive the blessing in quite a different way from what he was expecting it. Persons who "set their stakes," as the saying is, as to some certain way the Lord is to bestow his blessings upon them, are almost sure to have to pull up their "stakes," and become willing to accept it in any way the Lord sees fit to give it.

Faith is the key which unlocks the great treasure house of the Lord, and causes his blessings to shower down in abundance. To the Christian it is a shield which wards off the darts of the enemy; it removes mountains of opposition and discouragements, and brings a halo of glory about the soul, and the evil one is defeated on every hand.

It is a blessed thing to realize that our faith reaches unto Jesus Christ; for he is the end of our faith and is always ready to honor the same by an immediate answer.

CHAPTER VII.
CONVERSION.

Conversion is that change wrought in the soul which changes it from a natural to a spiritual state; from a sinful state to a state of grace. It is regeneration; a new or spiritual birth. It is an instantaneous work, wrought by the power of God which brings a person into a justified relation with God. It is as radical a change as is the natural birth of an infant. A new world to the soul has been reached, a new parentage given, and a heavenly parental arm of love is encircled round about with a wall of salvation to protect the new-born babe in Christ from the fiery darts of the evil one.

But how to solve this great problem and enable the soul to reach the desired haven of tranquillity and peace with God has been the great question of all enlightened people throughout the Christian era.

We are first to believe the Word of God, then act on that belief, which, if we are sinners, will at once bring about the conversion of the soul. The Lord speaks the words of pardon and says, "Thy sins are forgiven; go and sin no more." The burden of sin rolls away, and the peace of God comes in and illuminates the soul. A new era begins, and everything seems changed. So effective is it that what was once pleasure now does not seem to have any attraction; and the things that were formerly hated are now looked upon with admiration, and observed with a holy reverence. A new birth has taken place, and the new-born babe in Christ goes forth to walk in the heavenly light of God's word, and begins to feast upon the manna which cometh from above.

This spiritual birth is something that sinners do not understand, and they cannot because they are unable to discern the spiritual mind. They see the change of life in those who have been born again, and in their own strength and own way begin to try to reason out the ways of salvation. What do they get? They get just such an experience as Nicodemus had,—an experience of morality, and not of salvation. He was quite a prominent, great religious teacher; a ruler among the Jews, and yet confessed his ignorance regarding the conversion of the soul. Christ very plainly told him that his profession and experience would not take him to heaven, and said: "Except a man be born again he cannot see the kingdom of God."—Jno. 3: 3.

There are too many Nicodemases throughout the land at the present time; persons who are religious teachers, and yet strangers to this heavenly birth.

A man may make up his mind to do right, and determine to make heaven his home, and at once begin to change his ways. He stops swearing, lying, defrauding his neighbor, restores that which he has stolen, leaves off his bad habits, gives of his goods to the poor, attends religious services regular, and people notice a great change in the man, and yet he is only a moral man; and because he has not repented of his sins and been born of the Spirit, Christ says such a one "cannot see the kingdom of God."

There is a vast difference between morality and salvation. Morality does not include salvation; it changes the habits, but does not change the nature. But salvation always includes morality in the strictest sense. This blessed experience can be reached and claimed as our own the very moment we fully decide to forsake all sin, and have repented of all sin and confessed the same to God.

When the soul is converted a person can go about singing, "O happy day! when Jesus washed my sins away." Indeed this is a happy state, for there is peace with God. "Therefore being justified by faith we have peace with God through our Lord Jesus Christ."—Rom. 5: 1. This gives access, or opens the way of entrance into the standing grace of sanctification.

CHAPTER VIII.
SANCTIFICATION.

The command to the converted person is to go on unto perfection, Heb. 6: 1, "for this is the will of God even your sanctification."—1 Thess. 4: 3.

"And the very God of peace sanctify you wholly; and I pray God your whole spirit and soul and body be preserved blameless unto the coming of our Lord Jesus Christ."—1 Thess. 5: 23.

All actual transgressions have been pardoned, but the inherited nature still remains, which is the groundwork of sin in the heart, and in times of temptation and provocation leads into sin. Entire sanctification cleanses all this out of the soul, and it is then that we can claim all the blessings extended to the righteous.

Some one may ask the question, Who can be sanctified? We answer, None but BELIEVERS; for Christ and his apostles never urged anyone but believers to accept this grace. To the sinners they always preached repentance. If persons desire to enter this grace they must first know positively that all their sins have been pardoned, and after they have borne fruit

OF SOUL AND BODY.

of the same, they are then ready to be purged, that they may bear more fruit; ready to offer their bodies a "living sacrifice," and receive the "abiding Comforter." Jno. 14: 16.

The longing soul, hungering and thirsting after righteousness, cries out with the Psalmist: "Purge me with hyssop and I shall be clean: wash me, and I shall be whiter than snow;" and can then "serve him without fear, in holiness and righteousness before him all the days of our life."

"To him that overcometh will I give to eat of the tree of life which is in the midst of the paradise of God," saith the Lord.— Rev. 2: 7.

O this precious overcoming grace! This places the spiritual condition of the soul on a plane with Adam before the fall, to " eat of the tree of life," to " eat of the hidden manna." Ver. 17.

Hear the words of the Lord again in Rev. 3: 12.— "Him that overcometh will I make a pillar in the temple of my God, and he shall go no more out." This is the standing grace spoken of in Rom. 5: 2. It is where we are kept from falling as long as our trust is in God; it is where we are hid in the secret of his presence, "under the shadow of the Almighty." Oh! who would not go on to perfection and obtain this pearl of great price, though it requires the loss of all the worldly pleasures of earth?

Sinners may pray in vain for this grace; hypocrites may pray in vain for it; persons who have once been converted, but have since lived an unholy life may pray in vain for it. Many believers often seek for it day after day, and time after time plead with God for deliverance from this "body of sin," but their prayers seem, from some unknown cause to them, to go unanswered. In such cases there may be various reasons for the withholding of such a blessing. Some are not willing to be refined in the crucible of God's word; to pass through the crucifixion, and let the "old man" die; or, in other words, have the evil or carnal nature destroyed out of the soul. Reputation often stands in the way; but you may plead and plead in vain, and unless all things are completely given up you will not receive the desired blessing. You may give up things in your own way as often as you wish, yet you will have to come to God's way, and offer a perfect offering, and when that is done and you are positive all is wholly given up and all is on the altar, you then can claim the blessing in spite of all the powers of the enemy, and go your way doubting nothing; for whatever touches the altar is made holy. You are the gift, Christ is the altar, and the altar sanctifies the gift. Matt. 23: 19.

A very small thing will hinder the answering of prayer. In olden times when a sacrifice was brought before the altar it was thoroughly examined, and if the least blemish was found it was rejected.

Put your will in line with the will of God with all humbleness of heart, and the blessing will be forthcoming; the purging fire of his holiness will be upon you and instantly burn out all dross, and the last remains of sin will be destroyed; and as this is done the soul reaches the spiritual land of Canaan, where the Lord fights the battles, and faith moves onward with victory on every side; because the promised Comforter has taken up his abode in the soul.

There are many theories regarding sanctification, as to when and how the experience is obtained; but a theory which does not harmonize with the Word of God is a false one. Some get the idea that no one can live holy in this life, and even consider it presumption to claim sanctification. They imagine it can only be obtained at, or just about the time of death, when the spirit takes its flight for its eternal abode.

What saith the scriptures about such theories? We read in 1 Thess. 4: 3 that it is the will of God, even your sanctification. The word *sanctification* has a twofold meaning. First, a consecration or a setting apart for a sacred use. Second, the act of God's grace which cleanses, or purifies the affections of men.

All opposers of holiness, when measured by the Word of God, are found to be either out-right professional sinners or hypocrites, and are without a hope of heaven unless they turn from their evil ways; for our Bible tells us, "Without holiness no man shall see the Lord."........And Jesus said, "Be ye holy for I am holy."........How holy must we be? We must reach the point of PERFECTED holiness, for he says, "Be ye therefore perfect even as your Father which is in heaven is perfect.".......Certainly that is meant for us while here in this life. After being delivered from sin we are to *"serve him without fear, in holiness and righteousness before him all the days of our life."*—Luke 1:75. Then if we obey God we will from this time on live holy lives.

In justification we receive a degree of holiness through the pardon of sins, and being set apart for the service of the Lord; but God's command is not fulfilled until the cleansing process of entire sanctification takes place, which purifies the soul and sweeps away all the dross of the carnal nature. This is a work of grace wrought in the soul, separate and distinct from that of pardon. The soul enters the Elysian fields of bliss, and feasts upon the unfathomable riches of His glory. This makes a person an overcomer in the household of faith, a valiant soldier of the Lord, with victory on every hand.

Even this experience does not free us from temptation and the trials of life. No, indeed; we may be as our Master, but not above him. He was tempted by the evil one, and surely we will not escape the tempter; but it is in our power to resist him, for the Lord has promised that with every temptation there will be a way of escape. Our Savior suffered reproach and passed through severe trials of life; and so must we patiently run the race that is set before us, for only those who endure unto the end shall wear the crown.

There may be times when the Lord sees fit to try our faith to the utmost in order to fit us for some future responsibilities, or strengthen us for coming trials through which we may have to pass. At one time the Savior felt as though he was forsaken, and cried out, "My God! my God! why hast thou forsaken me?" Yet he did not feel like turning from his state of purity, nor allow a shadow of doubt to throw open a door for sin to enter; nor did he in anywise cast away his confidence in the Father. O what a lesson to be learned here! and may His children early learn that when the dark clouds are hovering, the sun is always shining behind, ready to break forth and dispel the gloom. And when our spiritual sky is clouded with gloom, faith reaches even through the darkest cloud to the Sun of righteousness; and not a stain of sin is able to touch the soul as long as the shield of faith is held up to turn the darts of the enemy. A sanctified person will be persecuted, reviled, evil spoken of; no doubt, pronounced crazy, a fanatic, and such like; but the Lord gives grace to endure all this with perfect peace in the soul. And this it will do: It will fit a person for the race, for the holy warfare, by removing all worldly conformity and everything that is not in accordance with the Word of God. The wearing of gold, jewelry and worldly adornments will give place to plain, neat clothing. Tobacco, opium, morphine, whiskey, beer, and even tea and coffee will not be used any more to defile the holy temple of God."For ye are the temple of the living God." —2 Cor. 6: 16. It is a sure cure for drunkenness, and will completely take away and destroy the appetite for strong drink; and will do the same for any other bad habit. Yea, it sweeps all sectarianism out of the heart, and delivers a person out of all religious creeds of men, secret societies and abominations of this world. Some are ready to take exceptions to some of these statements, and say, "You are going a little too far; just leave off some of these things." Nay, we will go further and say, when persons have had the light of the teaching of the Word of God on these things, they cannot even live in a justified state with God and practice them. Sanctification cleanses the soul from the desire of all these things.

OF SOUL AND BODY.

The Lord has commanded in 2 Cor. 6: 14, saying, "Be ye not unequally yoked together with unbelievers." And we are to have no fellowship with the works of darkness.

In consecrating for sanctification all is laid upon the altar; the sacrifice is made complete, an offering of all we know, and all we do not know. We consecrate to walk in all the light God lets shine upon our pathway. The Bible is opened as a new book to us, and as we begin to understand the deep things of God, the light will shine so brightly within and about us that we will see many things to which we have been clinging or leaning upon which are not in harmony with the Word of God, and as we discover them, we say, "Amen, Lord, that was considered in the covenant as one of the things about which we did not know at the time; and there is no desire for it now, so away it goes." When you have attained unto this grace and are walking up to all the light you have, and discover that there are points wherein you must make improvements, it does not require a new consecration, but only moving up to the light as it flashes upon your pathway, for nothing has been taken off the altar, and you are now where you can grow in grace through a knowledge of the truth as it is taught in the Word of God.

But suppose you were now to get light on some

point, and see by the Word of God that it was wrong to continue as before regarding the same, and you refuse to measure up to the teaching on that point when it is made clear to you, then you break your covenant and go into darkness; for Christ says, "Walk while ye have the light, lest darkness come upon you."

To have full salvation is to have the same salvation the apostles had; and it is our privilege to have that salvation, and to have the same faith, and to perform the same manner of works that the apostles did; but we must get on the apostolic line. It is not found on the line of secret orders, nor sectism, but is found in Jesus Christ only. "He sets the members in the body as it pleaseth him." "And ye are complete in him." O what a glorious thing it is to be just where God would have us be! where we are not afraid to step out upon the promises of his holy word.

CHAPTER IX.
THE TWO WORKS OF GRACE.

We frequently meet with persons who ridicule the idea of sanctification and justification being two separate and distinct works of grace wrought in the soul. They claim that when they came to the Lord they offered themselves a living sacrifice, and were converted and wholly sanctified both at the same time; and say the apostles were not converted until the day of Pentecost. Others claim that no one is sanctified in this life, and think when we get so good that we do not sin any more, then the Lord has no more use for us here on earth.

We may respect a person for their belief if they are honest in it, but we dare not drink of their unbelief, or uphold them in it, when we know they are wrong, in order to win them over to the side of truth. But they should be shown the truth in the light of the Gospel, and when made plain to them, they do not dare reject the truth, for the Word teaches that we must "walk in the light or go into darkness." Right here is where so many lose the grace of God out of their souls; they see the light, and will not advance, and walk in it, and so they are left in darkness. True, it is hard for many who have not had their spiritual eyes opened, or have been steeped with false teaching, to understand the teachings of the Word of God. But in about all such cases, you will find a selfish, stubborn will of their own, which refuses to be brought into line and subjection to His will; and as their will is to a greater or less extent set in opposition to the will of God, they find great difficulty in understanding the deep things of his word, even though they may hear it preached or explained in the plainest possible manner. Then the way to discover and possess the rich jewels and treasures of the Word of God, is to get your will in line with his; let your heart be fixed upon him; be willing to walk according to the teachings of his blessed word.

We do not hesitate in making the assertion in the light of God's word, that justification and sanctification are two separate and distinct works of grace wrought in the soul. The first is the forgiveness of all actual transgressions, and the infusion of spiritual life by the grace of regeneration. The second, the *cleansing* from all unrighteousness, having the evil, inherited nature rooted out. This is taught all through the Bible. Christ and his apostles preached repentance before the day of Pentecost, and while Christ was with them, his disciples baptized many persons. Surely they did not baptize sinners; for the command was for them to repent and then be baptized. Neither were the apostles sinners, for he says, "Behold, I send you forth as sheep in the midst of wolves."—Matt. 10: 16. The scriptures here represent the people who are sinners, as the wolves, and the saved ones as the "sheep." It would be absurd to think that Christ would send a number of sinners to preach the Gospel, heal the sick, cast out devils, etc. No, indeed, only saved persons are his ministers. Thousands of people at the present time are trying to

OF SOUL AND BODY. 37

preach the Gospel, whom God has never called nor commissioned; consequently they become false teachers, and darken the understanding of their hearers, thus causing divisions, strife, etc., "having a form of godliness, but denying the power thereof; from such turn away." The minister whom the Lord commissions and sends forth, is endued with power from on high, and his teaching is in the demonstration of the Spirit and in accordance with the Word of God.

You remember in Luke 10: 17-20, that when the seventy returned, they rejoiced that devils were subject unto them, and Christ told them to rejoice because their names were written in heaven. Surely the names of sinners are not written in heaven; if so, it would be useless to preach repentance. We read of some who came humbly to Christ and he forgave them, and said, "Go and sin no more." This was before the day of Pentecost. The promise of the Father was the Holy Ghost, which was not given before the day of Pentecost as an abiding Comforter.

For a sinner to go out to preach the Gospel would not be in harmony with the Word, because the first teaching of the Gospel, was repentance for the forgiveness of sins. And if His apostles had not been converted when they went out to preach, the people would have told them that they had better get saved themselves first. To be a follower of Christ, one must be a believer in his word; and to be a believer, one must obey his commands; and to do this will bring about a conversion of the soul the first thing. Consequently all who believe on him according to his word, are born of God. A mere religious inclination of the mind, or head religion will not suffice, but it must emanate from the depths of the soul. "For with the heart man believeth unto righteousness, and with the mouth confession is made unto salvation." To settle down upon good resolutions and a religious inclination without a change of heart, will save no one. The Word teaches that only believers can receive the Holy Ghost. "And I will pray the Father and he shall give you another Comforter, that he may abide with you forever; even the Spirit of truth, whom the world cannot receive, because it seeth him not, neither knoweth him: but ye know him; for he dwelleth with you, and shall be in you."—Jno. 14: 16, 17. Here he says the "world" (sinners) cannot receive this Comforter, which is the Holy Ghost; but his disciples "know him," and he shall be in them. In Jno. 17 we find Jesus praying for the sanctification of his disciples, and those who believe in him. This prayer was answered. Acts 2: 1–4. And the promise which had been spoken of was given.

Paul in illustrating the condition of a person with this inherited nature, says, "When I would do good evil is present with me." But as we read further on in his experience we find him "crucified with Christ," abounding in His love continually, free from all the sinful lusts of the world. In Acts 19:1, 2, when Paul came to Ephesus he found certain disciples, and said unto them, "Have ye received the Holy Ghost *since ye believed?*" And they said they had not so much as heard whether there be any Holy Ghost. So it is to-day: many do not even know that there is a Holy Ghost, because they have been under teachers who taught them not the words of our Lord Jesus Christ. Others believe that they received him when converted. Well, that is contrary to the Word to have the Holy Ghost as an abiding Comforter at the instant of conversion.

Now let us see how it is to be obtained. When a sinner comes to Christ he offers himself "dead in trespasses and sins," and is made alive in Christ through the forgiveness of sins, or actual transgressions, and that act or work of grace gives *access* into a deeper experience—into standing grace. Rom. 5: 1, 2. Read Rom. 12: 1, 2, and see how this second grace is attained unto. Remember he is speaking *here* to *brethren*; and as they had already offered themselves "dead in trespasses and sins," and been made alive in Christ, now he commands them to offer their bodies a *living* sacrifice, etc., which no sinners can do because they have not been made alive in Christ. A sinner cannot offer himself a holy sacrifice, but must meet the requirements of the Word through repentance before he is in a condition to even make the consecration for perfect holiness of heart. Does a person not grow into sanctification? No; there is a growth in grace, but not *into* grace. Through sanctification we receive a moral change of our nature; therefore sanctification is not effected by growth, as growth never changes the nature of anything. After we get *into* grace then we can grow in grace. We must get into a room before we can roam around in it. Growth changes the dimensions or size of anything; but a work of grace changes the nature.

When our fore-parents were in the garden or Eden hey were in a state of perfect holiness, were on a plane with God; but when they committed sin they fell from their holy state, and through their sin and fall sin passed upon all men. And as the Psalmist says, " Behold, I was shapen in iniquity, and in sin did my mother conceive me." So we are brought forth into this world with an inherited sinful nature, although in a state of innocency until we reach the years of accountability, and are old enough to know right from wrong; then this evil nature causes us to commit sin.

OF SOUL AND BODY. 41

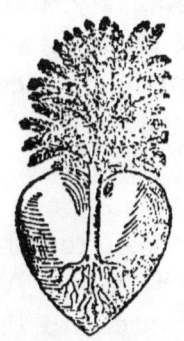
The Sinful Heart.

It is at this time that the sinful nature, which the enemy of souls planted in the heart at the time of the fall of man, causing him to be driven from the garden of Eden, now begins to develop as a tree and branch out, bearing fruits of wickedness, leading a person in forbidden paths and away from the innocency of early childhood. On account of this nature in the heart it is as natural a consequence for a child to drift into sin as it is for water to run down a hill. Although surrounding circumstances may do much to check the sinful career, yet a highly cultured life and strictest morality will never erase it. Nothing but the power of God will sweep it away and deliver one from its unholy tendency in the soul.

The Justified Heart.

Christ came to redeem us from sin, and make us pure and holy. Yes pure even as he is pure, for "as he is, so are we in this world." When our sins are forgiven it brings us into a justified state with God back to the innocency of childhood. This is the babe state of the Christian life. The new birth brings innocency and happiness, and opens the way to enter the realms of a deeper experience. As the soul gets a glimpse of the glories of entire sanctification there is a longing, a yearning for something more, a hungering and thirsting after righteousness. There is a lack unsupplied, a vacancy unfilled, and the soul cries out, "Cleanse me, O God, from this 'body of sin.'"

Through his cleansing blood we reach a point of moral perfection, and we are made to "sit together in heavenly places in Christ Jesus."—Eph. 2: 6. We cannot make the bound from a sinful state into that of entire sanctification all at one time. Why? Because it is not the Bible way, and what we do we must do as the Bible teaches.

There are many people who claim that when the Lord forgave their sins he also wholly sanctified them, and say that when he does a thing he does the whole thing at one time, and never makes two jobs of it. Such persons are certainly ignorant of the Word, and many have not even received the FIRST touch of his power. That is not the way God created the world. We also read in Mark 8: 22-26 about a blind man who was brought to Christ, and he spit on his eyes and laid his hands on him, and asked him if he could see. And the man said he could see men as trees walking. And Jesus after that put his hands again upon his eyes and made him look; and he was restored and saw every man clearly. So it is when we get our spiritual eyes opened through justification;

we then get a glimpse of perfected holiness, and when the cleansing takes place and our hearts purified completely, it is then that we are enabled to see clearly in the light of his word, and to rejoice with joy unspeakable and full of glory.

It is then that the last remains of sin are swept away, and the "old man" or "body of sin" is crucified and the Holy Spirit reigns supreme within the soul.

The Pure Heart.

In the Old Testament we find many types of the salvation of Jesus Christ, showing forth and typifying two works of grace, of which we will now notice one or two: First; it is plainly shown in the crossing of the Red Sea, and the river Jordan by the children of Israel. Their deliverance from Egyptian bondage, and escape through the Red Sea typifies our deliverance from sin by pardon through the blood of Jesus Christ. Their passing from the wilderness where they were daily fed on manna from heaven, across the Jordan into the land of Canaan, where they partook of the fruit of the land, typifies the passing from a justified into a sanctified state, where we can eat of the "hidden manna"

You will also observe that the Jewish tabernacle was a type of the true church of God; and by an outline of the same you will see that the offerings upon the

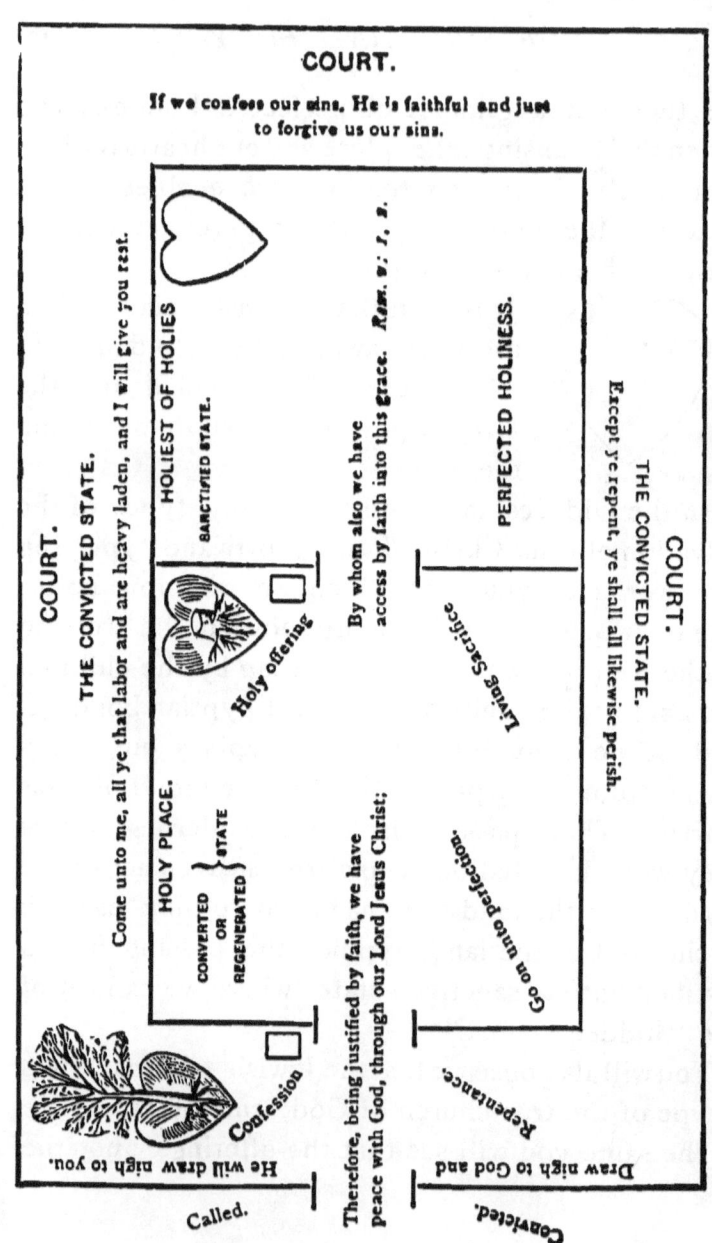

brazen altar admits into the first vail, or sanctuary, holy place; and the offering upon the golden altar, which admits into the second vail, or holiest of holies, corresponds with the offerings necessary to pass from sin unto entire sanctification. First, the sinner offers himself dead in tresspasses and in sins, and through the blood of Christ enters the kingdom, and is a child of the King, or in other words, is converted, having all actual transgressions or sins pardoned. "Therefore being justified by faith we have peace with God through our Lord Jesus Christ; by whom also we have access by faith into this grace wherein we stand, and rejoice in the hope of the glory of God."—Rom. 5: 1, 2.

Yet there remains in the heart that evil inherited nature, which the apostle sometimes called the "old man," the "root of bitterness," etc. And now as we have reached the point in our experience where we have access into a deeper experience, it is our privilege to have this "body of sin," or evil nature, with all its roots plucked up and destroyed. "For every plant which my heavenly Father hath not planted shall be rooted up."—Matt. 15: 13. And this is one of the plants which our heavenly Father hath not planted, consequently must be rooted up.

Now comes the second offering, a "living sacrifice." Paul says, Rom. 12: 1, 2,—"I beseech you therefore, brethren, by the mercies of God, that ye present your bodies a living sacrifice, holy, acceptable unto God, which is your reasonable service. And be not conformed to this world, but be ye transformed by the renewing of your mind, that ye may prove what is that good and acceptable and perfect will of God." " For this is the will of God, even your sanctification." —1 Thess. 4: 3.

What does this consecration include? When you first came to the Lord imploring him to forgive your sins, your case was a desperate one: all was darkness around you, and you were lost in sin. But you had to consecrate to God, that is, make a covenant with him—that you would forsake your sins; and then when you confessed all to him, you had to believe that he forgave you, because he promised in his word that " if we confess our sins he is faithful and just to forgive us our sins." Having now reached this experience we have peace with God, and can go on our way rejoicing that our sins are forgiven; but we have not yet reached that point where the inbred sin, or evil nature has been swept away. But having been made alive in Christ we can now make the offering —a "living sacrifice," and this does not require a confession of sins committed, but of indwelling sin, and results in a cleansing which sweeps away the inherited evil nature, leaving none of the elements of anger, strife, malice, filthiness of the flesh, etc. All the evil elements are removed, and O what a change! the Bible seems to be almost like a new book. The Holy Ghost takes up his abode in the soul and remains as our comforter, our guide, imparting wisdom, knowledge, etc. unto us, and the light of heaven shines about us in brilliant rays of glory, and his glorious presence is felt continually. O what sweetness! What completeness! We can truly say, "It is more precious than rubies;" yea, "sweeter than the honey and the honeycomb." Though it may be our lot to pass through the fiery furnace of affliction, or the deepest trials of life, forsaken by friends, an outcast, persecuted; and with all this the peace of the wholly sanctified is not destroyed, or even disturbed. Even though falsely accused and cast into prison, or led to the stake to be tortured and burned as a martyr, His grace will be sufficient even unto the end. To his faithful children it is glory all the way along. They who go on unto perfection and are willing to measure up to the Word of God in all things shall be possessors of the martyr's grace, and be able to stand all the fiery trials of life with a shout of victory in the soul.

When life's frail vessel is tempest tossed upon the rolling billows of oppression, and trouble and temptation are on every side, and the fiery darts of the enemy come thick and fast, these words are very precious to the one who leans upon the strong arm of the Lord: " When thou passest through the waters I will be with thee; and through the rivers, they shall not overflow thee: when thou walkest through the fire, thou shalt not be burned; neither shall the flame kindle upon thee, for I am the Lord thy God, the Holy One of Israel, thy Savior. * * * Fear not;for I am with thee."–Isa. 43: 2–5. " I will never leave thee nor forsake thee." Although to some who would look for a moment at their own strength, it may seem like such a severe trial would be more than their faith would be able to stand; but in turning to the precious promises of the Lord there is to be found the consoling words: " My grace is sufficient;" " Lo, I am with you alway, even unto the end of the world;" and " There hath no temptation taken you but such as is common to man: but God is faithful, who will not suffer you to be tempted above that ye are able, but will with the temptation also make a way to escape, that ye may be able to bear it."

DIVINE HEALING OF THE BODY.

PART II.

CHAPTER I.
THE DOCTRINE OF HEALING.

AMONG the religious class of people of to day there are multitudes of skeptics, regarding faith healing, or healing of the body by the means set forth in the Word of God. Volume after volume has been written on the subject; an abundance of testimonies have been published and sent broadcast over the land; yea, people have been eye-witnesses to the healing of the sick, yet in the face of all this, many will not believe.

We do not base the doctrine of divine healing upon the testimonies of those who have been healed in these last days; nor upon what has been written in many of the volumes published, for there is a more solid foundation upon which to build. The

Word of God is the true basis upon which its principles are founded, and it is presented in the strongest terms from Genesis to Revelation. Then what if some do not believe? "Shall their unbelief make the faith of God without effect? God forbid: Yea, let God be true, and every man a liar."—Rom. 3: 3.

The ways of the Lord are beyond the wisdom of men, and the heights and depths of his glory and mercies cannot be fathomed by human reasoning. Yet they cannot be questioned when viewed from a standpoint of reason and logic, when we take into consideration the infinite power and majesty of God, and that he is "all and in all," "The same yesterday, to day and forever.'

God who worked miracles in times past, still retains the same power, and will work through his true children and none can hinder.

Those who try to study out a way to heaven, or the principles of divine healing, through some scientific method will make a failure, unless they broaden their science enough to accept the miraculous performances of His power, and fall in line with the teachings of His word. They may harmonize the parting of the waters of the Red Sea by the blowing of an east wind, but when the river Jordan is reached, with its overflowing banks, and as the priests who bear the ark step into the water, which immediately parts and banks up on one side of them, and on the other side the river bed is left dry, a performance is witnessed which scientists fail to show any natural principles by which it was done; but are forced to admit that He who created the world, was able to separate the waters in any way he saw fit to do, whether it harmonized with science or natural laws or not.

Abraham understood upon what grounds this doctrine was founded, when he prayed for Abimelech whom the Lord healed. So did Moses when he prayed for the healing of Miriam, who had been stricken with leprosy, but through his prayer was restored. The other patriarchs of old, the holy prophets, and devout men of God, witnessed the healing of the sick by the power of God, and were instruments in his hands to perform wonderful things before the people.

The promise of the Lord to Moses and the children of Israel, if they would obey the voice of the Lord, was: "I will take sickness away from the midst of thee."—Ex. 23: 25. "I will put none of these diseases upon thee, which I have brought upon the Egyptians: for I am the Lord that healeth thee."—Ex. 15: 26. "Observe and hear all these words which I command thee, that it may go well with thee, and with thy childen after thee forever, when thou doest that which is good and right in the sight of the Lord thy God."—Deut. 12: 28. The promise, "Unto their children forever," reaches down to the present day. When God's children obeyed his voice these promises were fulfilled; when they disobeyed him the promises were not fulfilled.

Centuries after the above promises were given we hear the psalmist David breaking forth in these words: "Bless the Lord, O my soul, and forget not all his beneefits; who forgiveth all thine iniquities; who healeth all thy diseases."--Psa. 103: 2, 3.

When Hezekiah was "sick unto death," he prayed unto the Lord, a fervent prayer, and the same was answered by the healing of his body, and fifteen years were added unto his life. 2 Kings 20: 1-6. But in 2 Chron. 16: 12 we read of Asa, one of the kings of Israel, who sought not the Lord during his sickness, but put his case into the hands of earthly physicians, and the consequence was he died. In those days it was safe for the children of God to trust in Him for the healing of their bodies; and coming down to the time of Christ we find Him healing all manner of disease, "That it might be fulfilled which was spoken by Esaias the prophet saying, Himself took our infirmities, and bare our sicknesses."—Matt. 8: 17. Likewise His apostles went forth healing the sick, and doing wonderful things in the name of Jesus, and their work was wrought by the power of God. So we find the doctrine of divine healing is no new doctrine, as it is a part of the Word of God, and it has been the privilege of his faithful children in all ages of the past to claim his promises, and be healed of their diseases.

CHAPTER II.
IS THE DAY OF HEALING PAST?

We may as well ask, Has the Word of God become of none effect? or has God lost his power, insomuch that he cannot fulfill his promises? Professing Christians of to day are to be found in great numbers, who say the day of healing is past; it was for the apostles but not for us. But they fail to give us a "thus saith the Lord," for such a belief. Not one passage of scripture can be given to show that these promises were ever repealed, and that those who obey God have no right to claim them and be healed now. If we limit the healing power to the time of the apostles, and say it stopped there, then we must say the same regarding the salvation of the soul, for his word gives no more evidence of one having been done away, than it does the other.

Christ in giving his commission to the apostles said to them, " Go ye into all the world and preach the Gospel to every creature. He that believeth and is baptized shall be saved; but he that believeth not shall be damned; and these signs shall follow *them that believe:* In my name shall they cast out devils; they shall speak with new tongues; they shall take up serpents; and if they drink any deadly thing, it shall not hurt them; *they shall lay hands on the sick, and they shall recover.*"—Mark 16: 15-18.

Who shall lay hands on the sick?

"*Them that believe,*" shall lay hands on the sick, and they shall recover. Thank the Lord! We are of those who believe, consequently that promise is for us, and is for God's obedient children of to day. In James 5: 13-15, we not only have a promise but directions which is our duty to obey. "Is any among you afflicted? let him pray. Is any merry? let him sing psalms. Is any sick among you? let him call for the elders of the church; and let them pray over him, anointing him with oil in the name of the Lord: and the prayer of faith shall save the sick, and the Lord shall raise him up."

Because these things have been practiced but very little for the last few centuries does not change the Word of God in the least. Even if we knew of no cases of healing in these days, the Word would stand just the same, ready to be complied with, and followed by "these signs." The great trouble is with the people, and not with God; unbelief has found its way into their hearts, and false teachers have gone forth declaring the day of miracles past, and that God does not heal people of their diseases now, by the means set forth in his word, as he did in ancient times. But such persons fail to give one scripture to prove that such is the case.

As long as God has any obedient children upon earth it will be their privilege to call upon him, and according to the promises given in his word, be healed of their diseases; and not one passage of scripture can be found in the Bible to the contrary, or showing that these promises have been recalled. It would then be according to reason and logic to conclude that they are still in vogue, even if no one had the faith to claim them: but notwithstanding the unbelief of the masses of people, the true children of God have begun to realize the truth of his word, in spite of false teachers, and discern the body of Christ (the church),worshiping God in the beauty of holiness; exercising the gifts which Paul said "Covet earnestly."

Let us see if there is any more evidence that we have the right to perform miracles in these days, in the name of Jesus, and to follow the teachings of his word. Hear the words of Jesus: " Verily, verily. I say unto you, He that believeth on me, the works that I do, shall he do also; and greater works than these shall he do; because I go unto my Father. And whatsoever ye shall ask in my name, that will I do, that the Father may be glorified in the Son. If ye shall ask anything in my name I will do it." —Jno. 14: 12–14. Now these promises are to "He that believeth."

A man once told me that he did not believe in divine healing in these days; it was for the apostles and not for us. Said I, You believe the Bible, do you not? Oh, yes, every word of it, he remarked. Then what about such scriptures as these: "If ye abide in me, and my words abide in you, ye shall ask what ye will, and it shall be done unto you."—Jno. 15: 7. "If two of you shall agree on earth as touching anything that they shall ask, it shall be done for them of my Father which is in heaven."—Matt. 18: 19. Now suppose we are abiding in Christ, and should ask him to heal some one who is sick; would he not, according to his word, be under obligations to answer the prayer by doing the work, if we have faith in him? If that does not refer to our times, and these promises are not for us, then the Bible is a dead letter to us, and we may just as well throw the whole thing away.

He was then refered to the case of his daughter, with whom he had been visiting, who had been lying upon her bed for a week, very sick, and in an almost helpless condition; and a few days previous to our conversation, through prayer and by the laying on of hands, she was instantly healed, insomuch that she arose from her bed and immediately walked, praising God, and was healed of all disease from that moment, and received much strength to her body; yet it was several days before her strength was completely renewed; and because of this, her father doubted her healing. In order to substantiate his doubts he referred to another person for whom prayer had been offered, who was very near death's door, and because the afflicted one was not instantly restored to his normal strength, and new flesh put upon his bones, this man remarked that Christ never did his work by halves in that way, and never made but one job of anything. To this statement he was referred to the healing of the blind man. (Mark 8: 22–26.) Christ took the blind man by the hand and led him out of the town; and when he had spit on his eyes, and put his hands upon him, he asked him if he saw aught. And he looked up and said, I see men as trees, walking.

After that he put his hands again upon his eyes, and made him look up: and he was restored, and saw every man clearly. Also when the nobleman came to Christ to have his child healed (Jno. 4: 46–54), Christ seeing his faith, said unto him, "Go thy way; thy son liveth." And from that very hour the child began to amend. That does not intimate that the child was raised up at that hour, or that an abundance of strength was given, and new flesh put upon its bones, but simply states that it began to amend at that hour, that is, the disease was rebuked, and from that time it began to get better.

The Pharisees of old would not believe, even when Christ himself stood before them and performed miracles in their sight; just so at the present time people refuse to believe the truth when presented in all its purity; refuse to acknowledge the miraculous works of the Lord when they are eye-witnesses to the performance. Such denials and unbelief do not give the least evidence that the day of healing is past. O what a faithless people! who try to limit the power of God, and overthrow the faith of others. We are exhorted to "earnestly contend for the faith which was once delivered unto the saints.

"Many are the afflictions of the righteous: but the Lord delivereth him out of them all."—Psa. 34: 19 It is true that these bodies must sooner or later re turn to mother dust, for "it is appointed unto men once to die, but after this the judgment."—Heb. 9: 27. Yet, even this death may be stayed, through prayer and faith, for a number of years. (See 2 Kings 20: 6.) (1 Kings 3:14.) Many cry unto the

Lord in their afflictions, but on account of vanity and pride are not heard, while others are humble, yet are afraid to exercise faith because they cannot see the results first. They who walk only by sight do not walk by faith, because faith reaches beyond human vision and firmly grasps things unseen.

CHAPTER III.
THE USE OF DIVINE HEALING.

Everything in the divine economy is for a wise purpose, and is consonant with the highest reason.

Before entering upon the objects of divine healing it might be well to enquire briefly into the uses of affliction. And this must be approached by first considering the author of afflictions. Peter's testimony of Christ is as follows: "Who went about doing good, and healing all that were oppressed of the devil; for God was with him."—Acts 10: 38. Here afflictions are ascribed to the devil, to his oppressive power over human flesh. Doubtless, they are usually the result of violated natural laws through evil lusts and carelessness, infused by the devil. His object in these afflictions, of course, is to break down and destroy these temples of God. But God also has a permissive will and purpose in men's afflictions. By these afflictions upon his children he has taught them many profitable lessons, and brought them nearer to himself, and they have also thereby learned to hold more sacred and obey more carefully the laws that God has enacted in the realms of nature. Doubtless souls have been saved, and others arrested from apostasy by the strong hand of God in affliction. There have been instances where God has evidently sent physical judgments upon men. But these are exceptional. Usually disciplinary suffering is the effect of violated organic laws. But whatever gracious fruit sickness may bring forth, it is not to the glory of God that his children should continue long under its prostrating power. If a more perfect conformity to natural laws is needed, or if spiritual lessons or advancement in divine grace is the divine object in permitting those attacks, let the soul draw nigh to God, find out His good purpose, and reach the same. And when this is accomplished the divine use of the afflictions terminate, and the afflictions should also. But should no special blessing be contemplated, and the suffering be only the oppressive work of Satan, why should it be protracted? "Is there no balm in Gilead?" Is not our God able to deliver his children out of all trouble and afflictions? "Wherefore then should the heathen say, Where is their God?" Let it be known that God is indeed with his people, and is a present help in every need.

OF SOUL AND BODY.

What good then can the Lord accomplish in the exercise of his healing power? We will only mention a few things.

1st. Health is the normal state of man, an important condition of his usefulness. Deprived of this he is unable to answer the end of his active existence. He is not qualified to meet the duties he owes to himself as a man; to his conntry as a citizen; to society as a neighbor; to his family as a husband and father; nor to his God as a Christian. Not that he cannot be a Christian in prostration, but that he cannot fill the sphere of active Christian labor. Instead of filling life's duties in these several relations, he is a care and burden to others. Hence it is to the glory of God to heal His children, that Satan be defeated, and they be able to bring forth fruit unto God.

2d. By the exercise of his healing power, in answer to prayer, the Lord manifests unto his creatures his precious attributes of sympathy, compassion and love. Behold his heart of love toward suffering humanity! "And Jesus went forth and saw a great multitude, and was *moved with compassion* toward them, and he healed their sick."—Matt. 14: 14. Blessed be his dear name! Wherever his eyes beheld the oppressed of Satan, beneath the heel of sorrow and affliction, his hand of love was stretched forth to heal, and his kind heart overflowed with words that soothed the troubled soul. Had he passed through this vale of sin-inflicted wretchedness with no eye to pity the suffering, no tears to shed with the bereaved, and no outstretched arm to raise up the sick, could men have learned that his heart is kindness, and his Father's name love? Ah, the healing mercies of the Son of God are needful to reveal the character of that compassionate God, who only can bind up our wounds, heal our sorrows, and sweep away all our diseases.

And who will say that his crucifixion, resurrection and glorification have stripped him of his power to heal the sick? Nor do the glories of his Father's throne, and the lofty praises of the angels in heaven turn away his pitying eye from the pangs that oppress his frail brethren yet in the flesh, nor prevent their humble prayers from reaching his ears. Thank God! "He knoweth our frame and still remembers that we are dust." He yet walks with his church, showing forth even 'greater works' than he did while incarnate. He is near to all them that call upon him, and his tender mercies are over all. While on earth he turned no sufferer away unhealed, and his heart is no less "touched with the feelings of our infirmities" to day. All must admit that he has the same power to heal. Then why not do it? The person who could stand by the side of an awful sufferer, who is imploring

OF SOUL AND BODY.

help, and having all power and authority to remove the same by a simple touch and would not do it, what would be thought of such a person? Would not all pronounce his a heart of stone? And do not all who confess that Christ is able to heal his saints, and yet will not answer their prayers in doing so, virtually ascribe to him this same cruel, unfeeling heart? Do they not, in direct opposition to the Word, picture him as an unsympathizing high priest, whose heart cannot be touched with the feeling of our infirmities, and not even with the most intense pain and sickness? O my Lord and Savior, how thy name is dishonored, and thy holy character slandered by the false doctrines of men! How the cursed unbelief that has come down from the dark ages of confusion, and spread forth from the pulpits of worldly wisdom, and godly ignorance, robs our blessed Redeemer of his loveliness and tender compassion!

It is not enough to say that he exhibited his love to suffering humanity while in the flesh, and that is sufficient. Is it sufficient to prove that a man is good and holy now because he gave evidence of that fact in past years? If Christ cannot or would not heal the sick to day, would it not give place for doubts that he ever did, and that those miracles on record were forged? Surely this, or the ridiculous idea that he has changed. Though men may intellectually credit the works of Christ wrought over eighteen hundred years ago, to really impress their minds with his true character of love, they need to see the same manifestations in the present ever living Jesus. If he be indeed the divine Savior, "Jesus Christ the same yesterday, to day and forever," he must continue to confirm his love to his saints; and so he does. And he that denies it must shut his eyes and stop his ears from seeing and hearing the gracious works of God, and seek to rob him of his power, or of his very essence—love.

3d. We will notice one more point in the use of divine healing. In the name of the Lord we affirm that the supernatural healing of the bodies of men, is one of the Lord's permanent factors in the salvation of souls.

During the personal ministry of Christ, nearly all who believed in him were constrained to do so by the miracles they saw. Yea, " Many believed on his name when they saw the miracles which he did."— Jno. 2: 23. Those miracles were usually those of healing.

The same was true of the apostles' labors. About five thousand souls were converted to God through the preaching of a half sermon, which was backed up by the healing of a poor beggar at the beautiful gate of the temple. See Acts 3 and 4: 1-4. But since

OF SOUL AND BODY. 65

divine healing has been repudiated in the dark ages of the past, it has taken, on an average, about five thousand "fine sermons" to half convert one soul.

After spending the night in prison, and being tried by the high priests the next day, the apostles Peter and John were permitted to return to their own company and report the good time they had enjoyed, after which they all bowed down and prayed as follows: "And now, Lord, behold their threatenings, and grant unto thy servants, that with all boldness they may speak thy word, by stretching forth thy hand to heal; and that signs and wonders may be done by the name of thy holy child Jesus."—Acts 4: 29, 30. These inspired apostles knew how to pray for boldness and authority to preach the Word; namely, they wanted the hand of God manifest with them, confirming the Word with miracles, especially the healing of the sick. Do we not need the same boldness and authority to day? A ministry that is void of the divine seal of healing power is a poor, lame excuse for the messengers of the Almighty God.

Observe the use the Lord made of a case of healing at Lydda. Peter there "found a certain man named Æneas, which had kept his bed eight years, and was sick of the palsy. And Peter said unto him, Æneas, Jesus Christ maketh thee whole." You see Peter did not heal the man, but Jesus did. "And he arose immediately. And all that dwelt in Lydda and Saron saw him, and turned to the Lord."—Acts 9: 33-35. A very happy effect indeed. And we have seen men and women melt down before God and get saved in these last days, on seeing the love and power of God displayed in instantaneous healing.

"The day of miracles is past" is a digusting apology for an unsanctified and powerless ministry. It is much more congenial to the flesh to adopt this falsehood than to mortify the deeds of the body, die to all pride, selfishness and worldliness, and thus become pure in heart, and filled with power, an instrument through which God can bless suffering humanity.

The apostle Paul did not entertain the popular view of miracles so often heard from the faithless pulpits of our age; namely, that "they were only intended to confirm the divinity of Christ and his word, hence passed away with the apostles. "For," says he, "I will not dare to speak of any of those things which Christ hath not wrought by me, *to make the Gentiles obedient*, by word and deed, through mighty signs and wonders, by the power of the Spirit of God." —Rom. 15: 18, 19.

To make the Gentiles obedient to God, he regarded as the divine object of miracles. So long therefore as sinners are to be subjected to God on earth, the original object of healing yet remains, and of course the gracious gift continues in the church, even until the end of time. To this end the Lord commissioned supernatural healing in connection with the preaching of his word to the end of the world. Mark 16: 15–18. And for the same reason he set the gift of healing in the body, his church, as a permanent agent in the plan of salvation. 1 Cor. 12:.9. But observe he only put those gifts in his own church. Hence when men went from the divine fold and the faith once delivered to the saints, to human organisms, these signs did not follow. And to excuse their impotency the falsehood was coined that God had recalled that gift. But since the return of the holy remnant to the real Zion of God, the church of the first-born which are written in heaven, all these primitive gifts are found yet just where God placed them, and they are again being used to the glory of his name.

CHAPTER IV.
OLD TESTAMENT WITNESSES.

As we have already shown that it was the privilege of God's children in all ages to enjoy the blessings of divine healing of the body, we will now notice a few instances of the same, and wonderful faith and trust in God as given in his word. Beginning with the patriarchs of old, we read in Gen. 20: 17 that Abraham prayed unto God; and God healed Abimelech and his family. Also the prayer of Isaac, Gen. 25: 21. And of Jacob.—Gen. 30.

In Exodus 8-11 chapters we read of the power of God wrought through Moses by bringing the ten plagues upon Pharaoh and staying them at his command. Afterwards of the parting of the waters of the Red Sea that the children of Israel passed through upon dry ground; the smiting of the rock which brought forth water to quench the thirst of the people.

At one time when the people spoke against God and against Moses, "The Lord sent fiery serpents among the people, and they bit the people; and much people of Israel died. Therefore the people came to Moses and said, We have sinned, for we have spoken against the Lord, and against thee; pray unto the Lord that he take away the serpents from us. And Moses prayed for the people, and the Lord said unto Moses, Make thee a fiery serpent, and set it upon a pole: and it shall come to pass that every one that is bitten, when he looketh upon it shall live. And Moses made a serpent of brass and put it upon a pole, and it came to pass that if a serpent had bitten any man, when he beheld the serpent of brass, he lived."
—Num. 21: 6-9. It was through an act of faith that the people were healed of the wounds of the deadly serpent, for unless their belief was strong enough to

induce them to "look and live," they would perish.

At the present time the people have one to whom they can "look and live." For, "As Moses lifted up the serpent in the wilderness, even so must the Son of man be lifted up: that whosoever believeth in him should not perish, but have eternal life." And this same Jesus offers to heal all manner of disease, and give us whatsoever we ask in faith believing.

In the case of Hezekiah we have a witness to the wonderful manifestations of the power of the Lord in the healing of diseases, and the prolonging of life even after the prophet of the Lord had told him that the time had come for him to die.

"In those days was Hezekiah sick unto death. And the prophet Isaiah, the son of Amoz, came to him, and said unto him, Thus saith the Lord, Set thine house in order; for thou shalt die, and not live. Then he turned his face to the wall, and prayed unto the Lord, saying, I beseech thee, O Lord, remember now how I have walked before thee in truth and with a perfect heart, and have done that which is good in thy sight. And Hezekiah wept sore; and it came to pass, afore Isaiah was gone out into the middle court, that the word of the Lord came to him, saying, Turn again and tell Hezekiah, the captain of my people, Thus saith the Lord, the God of David thy father: I have heard thy prayer, I have seen thy tears: behold, I will heal thee: on the third day thou shalt go up unto the house of the Lord· And I will add unto thy days fifteen years."—2 Kings 20: 1–6.

The prophet Elisha was a man of God, known as such wherever he went. His fame was spread abroad throughout the land because of his wonderful power with God. Through his fervent prayers and close walk and communion with God he was enabled to perform miracles in the sight of men; such as raising the dead to life; parting the waters of Jordan by smiting them with the mantle of Elijah; causing iron to swim; confounding kings and armies, and many other things which only could be done through the power of God. The following instances are among the many wonderful manifestations of His power wrought through His servant, the first of which is the raising of the Shunammite's son.

THE WIDOW'S SON RESTORED TO LIFE.

"And when the child was grown, it fell on a day, that he went out to his father to the reapers. And he said unto his father, My head, my head! And he said to a lad, Carry him to his mother. And when he had taken him, and brought him to his mother, he sat on her knees till noon, and then died. And she went up, and laid him on the bed of the man of God, and shut the door upon him, and went

OF SOUL AND BODY.

out. And she called unto her husband, and said, Send me, I pray thee, one of the young men, and one of the asses, that I may run to the man of God, and come again. And he said, wherefore wilt thou go to him to day? it is neither new moon, nor sabbath. And she said, It shall be well. Then she saddled an ass, and said to her servant, Drive, and go forward; slack not thy riding for me, except I bid thee. So she went and came unto the man of God to mount Carmel. And it came to pass, when the man of God saw her afar off, that he said to Gehazi his servant, Behold, yonder is that Shunammite: Run now, I pray thee, to meet her, and say unto her, Is it well with thee? Is it well with thy husband? Is it well with the child? And she answered, It is well. And when she came to the man of God to the hill, she caught him by the feet: but Gehazi came near to thrust her away. And the man of God said, Let her alone; for her soul is vexed within her: and the Lord hath hid it from me, and hath not told me. Then she said, Did I desire a son of my lord? did I not say, Do not deceive me? Then he said to Gehazi, Gird up thy loins, and take my staff in thine hand, and go thy way: if thou meet any man, salute him not; and if any salute thee, answer him not again: and lay my staff upon the face of the child. And the mother of the child said, As the Lord liveth, and as thy soul liveth, I will not leave thee. And he arose and followed her. And Gehazi passed on before them, and laid the staff upon the face of the child; but there was neither voice, nor hearing. Wherefore he went again to meet him, and told him, saying, the child is not awaked. And when Elisha was come into the house, behold, the child was dead, and laid upon his bed. He went in therefore, and shut the door upon them twain, and prayed unto the Lord. And he went up, and lay upon the child and put his mouth upon his mouth, and his eyes upon his eyes, and his hands upon his hands: and he stretched himself upon the child; and the flesh of the child waxed warm. Then he returned, and walked in the house to and fro; and went up, and stretched himself upon him: and the child sneezed seven times, and the child opened his eyes. And he called Gehazi, and said, Call this Shunammite. So he called her. And when she was come in unto him he said, Take up thy son. Then she went in, and fell at his feet, and bowed herself to the ground, and took up her son, and went out."—2 Kings 4: 18-37.

NAAMAN CLEANSED OF LEPROSY.

"Now Naaman, captain of the host of the king of Syria, was a great man with his master, and honorable, because by him the Lord had given deliverance unto Syria: he was also a mighty man in valor, bu

OF SOUL AND BODY.

he was a leper. And the Syrians had gone out by companies, and had brought away captive out of the land of Israel a little maid: and she waited on Naaman's wife. And she said unto her mistress, Would God my lord were with the prophet that is in Samaria! for he would recover him of his leprosy. And one went in, and told his lord, saying, Thus and thus said the maid that is of the land of Israel. And the king of Syria said, Go to, go, and I will send a letter unto the king of Israel. And he departed, and took with him ten talents of silver, and six thousand pieces of gold, and ten changes of raiment. And he brought the letter to the king of Israel, saying, Now when this letter is come unto thee, behold, I have therewith sent Naaman my servant to thee, that thou mayest recover him of his leprosy. And it came to pass, when the king of Israel had read the letter, that he rent his clothes, and said, Am I God, to kill and to make alive, that this man doth send unto me to recover a man of his leprosy? Wherefore consider, I pray you, and see how he seeketh a quarrel against me. And it was so, when Elisha the man of God had heard that the king of Israel had rent his clothes, that he sent to the king, saying, Wherefore hast thou rent thy clothes? let him come now to me, and he shall know that there is a prophet in Israel. So Naaman came with his horses and with his chariot, and stood at the door of the house of Elisha. And Elisha sent a messenger unto him, saying, Go and wash in Jordan seven times, and thy flesh shall come again unto thee, and thou shalt be clean. But Naaman was wroth, and went away, and said, Behold, I thought, he will surely come out to me, and stand, and call on the name of the Lord his God, and strike his hand over the place, and recover the leper. Are not Abana and Pharpar, rivers of Damascus' better than all the waters of Israel? may I not wash in them, and be clean? So he turned and went away in a rage. And his servants came near, and spake unto him, and said, My father, if the prophet had bid thee do some great thing, wouldst thou not have done it? how much rather then, when he saith to thee, Wash, and be clean? Then went he down, and dipped himself seven times in Jordan, according to the saying of the man of God: and his flesh came again like unto the flesh of a little child, and he was clean."—2 Kings 5: 1–14.

Here we find an instance of direct obedience to the commands of God, even in what would, and did seem to be very small and simple matters of instruction, which had to be carried out to the full extent of the directions given, before the work was accomplished. It was not enough for this captain to believe that he would be healed by making applica-

OF SOUL AND BODY.

tion to the prophet, but he had to go and wash himself seven times in the river Jordan. As he was a man of authority, he thought surely the man of God would come out and make a great ado over him; but on the other hand the prophet only sent a messenger and told him to go and wash in Jordan. This at first seemed to be too small a matter for him to perform; it was beneath his dignity and did not meet his anticipations; was just a little too humiliating, yet he had to come to the point where he would willingly obey, and as soon as he obeyed, and had dipped seven times, he was made every whit whole. Dipping in another river would not have sufficed; dipping six times only would have left him still a leper.

This instance of healing teaches us a lesson which we will find taught all through the Word of God, that to obtain healing through the power of God, we must obey his word by doing that which he has commanded. Under the present gospel dispensation there are professing Christians who almost abhor the idea of obeying James 5: 14, 15, by anointing with oil, and laying on of hands, and praying over the sick for their recovery. Where you find persons rejecting these commands, you will find they do not take God as their only physician. The virtue is not in the oil, any more than in the waters of

Jordan, but in Christ. When faith and works unite upon a line with God's word, then virtue goes forth and the work is accomplished, and the captive now set free can "stand still and see the salvation of the Lord," and shout victory over sin and disease.

CHAPTER V.
NEW TESTAMENT WITNESSES.

Turning to the New Testament, we find that foremost among the workers of miracles was Jesus: He who said, "All power is given unto me in heaven and in earth;" the incarnate Son of God, who was without sin, "neither was guile found in his mouth." The miracles wrought by him are so numerous that it is not necessary to give a detailed account of many of them, and by only referring to a few of them will be sufficient to show the most skeptic that his power was unlimited.

At the close of his sermon on the mount, Jesus came down from the mountain, and a leper came unto him, and as Jesus touched him, he was cleansed of his leprosy. Next he healed the centurion's servant of palsy, and did not even go to visit the servant, but only spoke the word and the work was done. He touched the hand of Peter's wife's mother and the fever left her.

OF SOUL AND BODY.

"When even was come, they brought unto him many that were possessed with devils: and he cast out the spirits with his word, and healed all that were sick: that it might be fulfilled, which was spoken by Esaias the prophet, saying, Himself took our infirmities, and bare our sicknesses."—Matt. 8: 1-17. In the following chapter we read of a certain ruler who had great faith in the power of Jesus, who came to him, saying,

"My daughter is even now dead: but come and lay thy hand upon her, and she shall live. And Jesus arose, and followed him, and so did his disciples. And, behold, a woman which was diseased with an issue of blood twelve years, came behind him, and touched the hem of his garment: For she said within herself, If I may but touch his garment I shall be whole. But Jesus turned him about, and when he saw her, he said, Daughter, be of good comfort; thy faith hath made thee whole. And the woman was made whole from that hour. And when Jesus came into the ruler's house, and saw the minstrels and the people making a noise, he said unto them, Give place: for the maid is not dead, but sleepeth. And they laughed him to scorn But when the people were put forth, he went in, and took her by the hand, and the maid arose. And the fame hereof went abroad into all that land. And when Jesus departed thence, two blind men followed him, crying, and saying, Thou Son of David, have mercy on us. And when he was come into the house, the blind men came to him: and Jesus saith unto them, Believe ye that I am able to do this? They said unto him, Yea, Lord. Then touched he their eyes, saying, According to your faith be it unto you. And their eyes were opened; and Jesus straitly charged them, saying, See that no man know it. But they, when they were departed, spread abroad his fame in all that country. And as they went out, behold, they brought to him a dumb man possessed with a devil. And when the devil was cast out, the dumb spake: and the multitudes marvelled, saying, It was never so seen in Israel. But the Pharisees said, He casteth out devils through the prince of the devils. And Jesus went about all the cities and villages, teaching in their synagogues, and preaching the gospel of the kingdom, and healing every sickness and every disease among the people."

Here we see that not only the dead was raised, but he healed "every sickness and every disease among the people;" "insomuch that the multitude wondered, when they saw the dumb to speak, the maimed to be whole, the lame to walk, and the blind to see: and they glorified the God of Israel."

These miracles of healing; the feeding of the five thousand; (Mark 6.) turning water into wine;

(Jno. 2.) stilling the storm; (Luke 8.) walking on the sea; (Matt. 16.) and many others show his supernatural power, yet when he called his disciples he gave them power to do the *same* things, and did not even limit the power to the apostles alone, but to those who would believe on him; for he said: "Verily, verily, I say unto you, he that believeth on me, the works that I do shall he do also; and greater works than these shall he do; because I go unto my Father. * * If ye shall ask anything in my name, I will do it."—14: 12-14.

"When he had called unto him his twelve disciples, he gave them power against unclean spirits, to cast them out, and to heal all manner of sickness and all manner of disease..... And as ye go, preach, saying, The kingdom of heaven is at hand. Heal the sick, cleanse the lepers, raise the dead, cast out devils; freely ye have received, freely give."—Jno. 10: 1-8. Mark 16: 15-18.

He gave a like commission to the seventy whom he sent forth, and when they returned they rejoiced on account of these things, but Jesus told them to rejoice that their names were written in heaven

In Jno. 14: 16, another Comforter was promised, which promise was fulfilled.—Acts 2: 4.

The scriptures have already been given showing the miraculous power of our Lord and Savior, and his command to his disciples to do the same things; and now we will give attention to what took place after the death of our blessed Savior. As they had before gone forth working miracles and preaching the kingdom, it seemed now that a double portion of power had been bestowed upon them, as "they were all of one accord in one place on the day of Pentecost, the Spirit gave them utterance to speak with such power and authority that the different nations of people were astonished at them, and Peter was not afraid to give them the plain truth, and expose the wickedness of the people.

Now followed a circumstance substantiating the words of Jesus, and showing his power through his children.

THE LAME MAN HEALED.

As "Peter and John went up together into the the temple at the hour of prayer, being the ninth hour, and a certain man lame from his mother's womb was carried, whom they laid daily at the gate of the temple which is called Beautiful, to ask alms of them that entered into the temple; who, seeing Peter and John about to go into the temple, asked an alms. And Peter. fastening his eyes upon him with John, said, Look on us. And he gave heed unto them, expecting to receive something of them.

OF SOUL AND BODY.

Then Peter said, Silver and gold have I none; but such as I have give I thee: In the name of Jesus Christ of Nazareth rise up and walk. And he took him by the right hand, and lifted him up: and immediately his feet and ankle bones received strength. And he leaping up stood, and walked, and entered with them into the temple, walking, and leaping, and praising God. And all the people saw him walking and praising God: and they knew that it was he which sat for alms at the Beautiful gate of the temple: and they were filled with wonder and amazement at that which had happened unto him. And as the lame man which was healed held Peter and John, all the people ran together unto them in the porch that is called Solomon's, greatly wondering."—Acts 3: 1-11.

Quite an excitement followed, which brought many people out to hear the Word of God preached and doubtless many came through mere curiosity; however the truth preached had its effect and about five thousand souls were saved. For this cause Peter and John were put in prison, and upon being released were threatened and warned not to teach in the name of Jesus any more. But they went in prayer and said: " Now, Lord, behold their threatenings; and grant unto thy servants that with all boldness they may speak thy word, by stretching forth thine hand to heal; and that signs and wonders may be done by the name of thy holy child Jesus." And in a very short time afterward, "they were all with one accord in Solomon's porch. And of the rest durst no man join himself to them; but the people magnified them. And believers were the more added to the Lord, multitudes both of men and women; insomuch that they brought forth the sick into the streets, and laid them on beds and couches, that at the least the shadow of Peter passing by might overshadow some of them. There came also a multitude out of the cities round about unto Jerusalem, bringing sick folks, and them which were vexed with unclean spirits: and they were healed every one."—Acts 5: 12-16. Jesus healed all those who were brought unto him that were sick, and here we find his disciples doing the same thing, for the Word says, "They were healed every one."

HEALED OF PALSY.—DEAD RAISED.

"And it came to pass, as Peter passed throughout all quarters, he came down also to the saints which dwelt at Lydda. And there he found a certain man named Æneas, which had kept his bed eight years and was sick of the palsy. And Peter said unto him, Æneas, Jesus Christ maketh thee whole: arise, and make thy bed. And he arose immediately. And all that dwelt at Lydda and Saron saw him, and turned to

OF SOUL AND BODY.

the Lord. Now there was at Joppa a certain disciple named Tabitha, which by interpretation is called Dorcas: this woman was full of good works and almsdeeds which she did. And it came to pass in those days that she was sick, and died: whom when they had washed, they laid her in an upper chamber. And forasmuch as Lydda was nigh to Joppa, and the disciples had heard that Peter was there, they sent unto him two men, desiring him that he would not delay to come to them. Then Peter arose and went with them. When he was come, they brought him into the upper chamber: and all the widows stood by him weeping, and shewing the coats and garments which Dorcas made, while she was with them. But Peter put them all forth, and kneeled down, and prayed; and turning him to the body said, Tabitha, arise. And she opened her eyes; and when she saw Peter, she sat up. And he gave her his hand, and lifted her up; and when he had called the saints and widows, he presented her alive. And it was known throughout all Joppa; and many believed in the Lord."—Acts 9: 32-42.

Many wonderful things were performed by the other apostles, also showing forth the power of God to heal the body and save the soul. And these manifestations of the power of God were always followed by much persecution, because it had a tendency to draw people to Christ, and also the enemies of the sacred truth of the Gospel, were stirred up often to violence of the worst kind. The disciples did not fear to preach the Gospel in all its purity, and with all plainness of speech declare the whole counsel of God, exposing the wickedness of evil doers and the horrors of sin. When Paul and Barnabas came to Iconium, the Lord "granted signs and wonders to be done by their hands," among which was

THE HEALING OF A CRIPPLE.

"And there sat a man at Lystra, impotent in his feet, being a cripple from his mother's womb, who never had walked. The same heard Paul speak: who steadfastly beholding him, and perceiving that he had faith to be healed, said with a loud voice, Stand upright on thy feet. And he leaped and walked."—Acts 14: 8–10.

SPIRIT OF DIVINATION CAST OUT.

When they went to Macedonia, Paul says, "It came to pass, as we went to prayer, a certain damsel possessed with a spirit of divination met us, which brought her masters much gain by soothsaying: the same followed Paul and us, and cried, saying, These men are the servants of the most high God, which shew unto us the way of salvation. And this did she many days. But Paul, being grieved, turned and

OF SOUL AND BODY. 85

said to the spirit, I command thee in the name of Jesus Christ to come out of her. And he came out the same hour."—Acts 16: 16-18.

Upon Paul's return to Macedonia, God again manifested his power through him, in a miraculous way in

RAISING THE DEAD.

"And there sat in a window a certain young man named Eutychus, being fallen into a deep sleep: and as Paul was long preaching, he sunk down with sleep, and fell down from the third loft, and was taken up dead. And Paul went down, and fell on him, and embracing him said, Trouble not yourselves; for his life is in him. When he therefore was come up again, and had broken bread, and eaten, and talked a long while, even till break of day, so he departed. And they brought the young man alive, and were not a little comforted."—Acts 20: 9-12.

At the time when they were shipwrecked and cast on the island of Melita, among a barbarous people, Paul "gathered a bundle of sticks and laid them on the fire; there came a viper out of the heat, and fastened on his hand. And when the barbarians saw the venomous beast hang on his hand, they said among themselves, No doubt this man is a murderer, whom, though he hath escaped the sea, yet vengeance suffereth not to live. And he shook off the beast into the fire, and felt no harm. Howbeit they looked when he should have swollen, or fallen down dead suddenly: but after they had looked a great while, and saw no harm come to him, they changed their minds, and said that he was a god. In the same quarters were possessions of the chief man of the island, whose name was Publius; who received us, and lodged us three days courteously. And it came to pass, that the father of Publius lay sick of a fever and of a bloody flux: to whom Paul entered in, and prayed, and laid his hands on him, and healed him. So when this was done, others also, which had diseases in the island, came, and were healed."—Acts 28: 3-9.

By reading the Word we find that the power to do such things was given to others besides the twelve apostles. In the tenth chapter of Saint Luke we find the seventy whom Christ sent forth were endued with the same power. And in the last chapter of Mark we find this power was given to "THEM THAT BELIEVE." It was through the faith of some of those believers that even the prison doors were opened and Peter set at liberty, for "prayer was made without ceasing of the church unto God for him."—Acts 12: 5. Many other testimonies might be given, but it is unnecessary, for in "the mouth of

OF SOUL AND BODY. 87

two or three witnesses shall every word be established." The command in the last chapter of Saint Mark, which was given to "them that believe," has never been done away with, and never will be as long as God has a people on earth who have faith enough to believe and obey his word. When the day of healing is past, and God refuses to fulfill those promises, rest assured that the day of faith will also be past, and salvation work will be at an end.

CHAPTER VI.
THE APOSTASY.

The Christian era is represented in the Word of God as a day,—a "day of the Lord," which dawned with all the brightness of the morning. The holy prophets of old foretold this notable time when Christ would establish his church upon the earth, and to those who would fear the name of the Lord would the "Sun of righteousness arise with healing in his wings." This "Sun of righteousnes'" was Christ, the light of the world; He who came to save the people from their sins and establish them in the ways of truth. He was a light to them that sat in darkness, and they who were willing to humble themselves and become his disciples, he gave power over devils and victory over the wickedness of this world. His disciples were of the "same mind," and saw "eye to eye," and through the name of Jesus they were enabled to perform miracles in the sight of men, and devils were made to "fear and tremble." The church of God was not a human organized concern then, any more than it is at the present day. Christ placed the members in the body as it pleased him. It is a "glorious church, not having spot or wrinkle, or any such thing."—Eph. 5: 27. And all the members are holy, and not one of them living in sin, because Christ is the door into this church, and nothing sinful can enter. The only way to get into God's church is to be born into it, and we are then in his family; a son of God; a child of the king; a branch of the true vine.

Having then been born of God, and already a member of his body, would it not be presumption to think of joining anything else in order to belong to the church, when we are already in the church the very moment we get salvation?

This church was founded upon Christ, the Rock of our salvation.— Matt. 16: 18. It is his body.— Col. 1: 24. And he is the head of it.—Col. 1: 18. He purchased it with his blood.—Acts 2: 20. Its name is the Church of God.—1 Cor. 10:32. The class book is kept in heaven.—Heb. 11: 24. Salvation then is the requirement which admits a person into the church. (Jno. 10:9.) And God places the members in the body as it pleases him (1 Cor. 12:13), bestowing such gifts upon them as they stand in need of, and all work in sweet harmony.

In the morning of this Christian era, the church had wonderful power; they met together "with one accord," and the power of God was wonderfully manifested in and through them, and many were added unto the church. The sick were healed, devils were cast out, and the Gospel preached in all its purity.

But as the years passed by, people began to depart from the faith, and bring in false doctrines, heresies, schisms, etc., causing divisions, just as Paul said would take place. This was the starting point of sectism. There had been no human organization or creed among God's people since the time of Christ; but now, like spirits, such as were fallen from grace, began to assemble together and by the help of Satan himself, tried to devise some plan to deceive souls, and drag them down to ruin. This state of affairs continued until the enemy of souls had devised a plan to destroy souls by the wholesale. Before three centuries had passed by, the ruling power of the church was centralized in the Bishop of Rome, and Roman Catholicism began to develop, and another important step was taken in the establishing of this creed, in the year 325, when the Nicene council was held. This sect, or "mother of harlots," as the Bible terms it (Rev. 17: 5), was called a church in order to better deceive souls; and the "man of sin" which Paul tells us will be made manifest, or revealed, is the papal power. People were forced, at the peril of their lives, to acknowledge the pope as the head of the church, and become submissive to the galling yoke of Catholicism, and renounce their former experience and belief. And those who would stand true to God, were martyred, or had to suffer the most appalling persecution, often "resisting unto blood," for the sake of Christ. The common people were denied the privilege of reading the Word of God. An awful time of spiritual darkness came upon the land; this was the time of which the prophets foretold, when the sun would go down at noon. The Sun of righteousness, or real church of God, seemed to be in obscurity, hid away behind the dark clouds of papacy: nevertheless God had true followers all through this time, who would not bow the knee to Baal; who preferred to obey God rather than man, and were hunted down and persecuted, and had to hide themselves in caves in order to worship God. But "truth crushed to earth shall rise again," and thus it proved in this great and severe ordeal through which the church had to pass. Yet it took centuries for it to

OF SOUL AND BODY.

gain what seemed from an outward appearance, a good foothold, in order to rise above the over-hanging clouds of the spiritual darkness.

After awhile, a daughter was born into the family of mystic Babylon; or, in other words, another sect was formed, a split from the old mother of harlots, and in a few centuries there was an abundance of daughters born into the family, each making a league with the devil to bring honest souls into bondage, and with their oath of allegiance to obey the rules of the family or creed, became "unequally yoked together with unbelievers," which the Word of God condemns.—2 Cor. 6: 14. It was not the intention of those good old reformers to enter into any league with the enemy in order to deceive souls. They saw the corruption of Romanism, and realized the judgments of God upon her, and thus made their escape, and not having sufficient light on the Word of God, their followers soon drifted into sectism, forming creeds one after another with the hope of bettering the condition of the church, not discerning the "body of Christ," the true church. Dear honest souls united with them, believing it to be the best thing they could do, and worshiped God with all their hearts. Notwithstanding God blessed the labors of those who faithfully trusted him, yet that was no evidence that sectism itself was right, for they were doubtless walking up to the light they had on the Word of God. But the time was not far distant when he would send forth his judgments against these schisms, and deliver his children out of them, revealing unto them the true church of the living God.

Sectism soon reached its highest point, each schism or creed claiming to be the church, a branch of the true vine. Each fighting the other, having conflicting views and doctrines of teaching, yet claiming to belong to that one body, the "church of the living God." O what darkness! what blindness! what soul-deceiving, soul-destroying nets and snares the enemy has prepared to capture the souls of men! This is the Babylon spoken of in Revelations. Babylon means confusion, and mystic Babylon is the spiritual confusion in the so-called churches of to day, which has been the means of making more infidels than have all the infidel writers during the past ages. Honest people give their hearts to God, and are invited and urged to join some of these so-called churches, "in order to have a home among God's people;" and read in their Bible of the unity of God's church, and begin to look about them, and find all the creeds arrayed, one against the other. The consequence is, many, when they find themselves thus duped, come to the conclusion that

OF SOUL AND BODY. 93

Christianity is a farce and a failure, and thus infidelity takes up its abode in the heart, and multitudes are led astray and lost throughout eternity. The departing from "the faith once delivered to the saints," was the beginning of sectism; was the beginning of the apostasy. From that time the church was shorn of its strength; what real honest souls were left were mostly joined to some branch of Babylon, and were not permitted to assert their liberty in Christ according to the Word of God, because of the rigid rules of their creed. Then came an awful famine throughout the land, a starving of souls, for want of spiritual food—the true bread of life. This famine is the one spoken of by the prophet Amos: "Behold, the days come, saith the Lord God, that I will send a famine in the land; not a famine of bread, nor a thirst for water, but a hearing of the words of the Lord."—Amos 8: 11. Truly this time has already come, and has been realized in the last few centuries. Ministers all over the land have become false shepherds, fleecing the flock and leaving them to starve. "Blind watchmen," according to Isa. 56: 9–12. "Having a form of godliness, but denying the power thereof: from such turn away."—2 Tim. 3: 5. Is it any wonder that spiritual darkness prevails throughout the land, when such doctrines are taught from the pulpit, the press, at home, and everywhere? With "fair words and smooth speeches," people are rocked to sleep (spiritually) right on the brink of hell, and seem to be unconcerned regarding the welfare of their souls; unawakened to their awful condition; joined to their idols; and because they were at ease in Zion— if they have ever advanced enough to enter her portals,—have become "lukewarm," and have been spewed out, because they were neither 'cold nor hot.'

O the famishing of souls! the pestilence of unbelief and deception! it is widespread, almost universal. Darkness covers the land, and the scene is too appalling to behold.

What has been termed the church, has long ago entered the bridal chamber with the world, and the devil officiating at the nuptial ceremony, sealing the service with a smile of approval, and best wishes that their happiness may continue and their fellowship never be broken. The happy bridal pair long ago entered upon their honeymoon, and as they travel along, bedecked alike in a gaudy dress of worldly fashions, many church socials, fairs, suppers, aristocratic parties, etc., are given in honor of the same, and there is a time of general festivity and revelry.

The all-seeing eye of God witnesses the scene, and he sends forth his messenger declaring with a strong voice, saying: "Babylon the great is fallen, is fallen, and is become the habitation of devils, and the hold of every foul spirit," etc.—Rev. 18: 2.

The great literal city of Babylon was taken in a time of festivity and revelry, while king Belshazzar was having a feast, and the people were drunken with wine. How true a type of the taking of spiritual Babylon, and her utter fall, while "all nations have drunk of the wine of the wrath of her fornication."—Rev. 18: 3. "Thus shall Babylon sink to rise no more."—Jer. 51: 64.

CHAPTER VII.
THE EVENING LIGHT.

"But it shall be one day which shall be known to the Lord, not day, nor night: but it shall come to pass, that at evening time it shall be light."—Zech. 14: 7.

"In that day there shall be a fountain opened to the house of David, and to the inhabitants of Jerusalem, for sin and uncleanness."—Zech. 13: 1.

"Awake, awake; put on thy strength, O Zion; put on thy beautiful garments, O Jerusalem, the holy city: for henceforth there shall no more come into thee the uncircumcised and the unclean."—Isa. 52: 1.

Amid all the spiritual confusion in these last days, God has a people, a "remnant," and the time has come when he is calling them together in the unity of his love. A holy people, a pure church, whose light cannot be hid, but shineth with the brightness of the morning. It was on account of their departing from the "faith once delivered unto the saints," that the Lord permitted his children to be taken captive in mystic Babylon; but he says, "Ye shall seek me, and find me, when ye shall search for me with all your heart; and I will be found of you, and will turn away your captivity, and will gather you from all the nations," etc.—Jer. 29: 14.

"Therefore thus saith the Lord, If thou return, then will I bring thee again, and thou shalt stand before me: and if thou take forth the precious from the vile, thou shalt be as my mouth: let them return unto thee; but return not thou unto them."—Jer. 15: 19.

The time has now come when God s true church—the bride of Christ—shines forth with all its splendor and beauty, fair as the noonday, bright as the morning, endued with strength and power from on high, as in the morning of the Christian era; "a glorious church, not having spot or wrinkle, or any such thing;" exercising the gifts of the Spirit as God intended from the beginning; free from the babylon confusion of sectism; clothed in the glorious robes of full salvation. The Lord is sending his messengers forth to the four winds of the earth gathering together the elect—his people—teaching them the oneness of Christ, and exposing the spiritual darkness and utter ruin of Babylon. In Rev. 18: 2, we read the doom of this mystic Babylon, and in verse 4 is a positive command to the children of God, saying, " Come out of her, my people, that ye be not partakers of her sins, and that ye receive not of her plagues."

Dear reader, this command is for you, if you are a child of God, and yoked up in some religious creed. If you are not a child of God, then rest assured that the command is not for you, and it is for you to choose, as to whether or not you will be classed with what is described in Rev. 18: 2. You may consider this strong language, but the salvation of your soul depends upon the obeying of the Word of God.

" My people, go ye out of the midst of her and deliver ye every man his soul from the fierce anger of the Lord."—Jer. 51: 45.

Go ye out of the midst of her; be ye clean, that bear the vessels of the Lord."—Isa. 52: 11.

In presenting these truths, we do not wish to be misunderstood, but desire to give light to the good people who are yet in sectism. There are many good honest souls in the different religious denominations of to day, longing for the time to come when God's people will all be "one," and united in the one body, as Christ prayed that they should be. Jno. 17: 21. The creeds of to day are seeking some plan upon which to unite, but fail, for the walls of division are still there. This holy union is found only in Christ. Behold, the time is now here for this oneness, and his children discern the real spiritual body of Christ—his church—and are bound together with love, instead of disciplines and rules of men.

This evening light is the shining forth of the true church, and Zion puts on her strength, and is no longer in obscurity, nor her people bound down with thongs of opinions; no longer to sing the songs of Zion in a strange land, but are brought into their "own land"—perfected holiness—which is the Canaan to the soul.

Sectism will continue as before, and her inhabitants go on professing godliness, deceiving and being deceived, but a line of demarkation will be drawn by the Word of God, which plainly points out the narrow way—the only way to heaven. We dare not falter; dare not refuse to walk in the light of the Gospel, for Jesus says: "Walk while ye have the light, lest darkness come upon you. * * * While ye have light, believe in the light."—Jno. 12: 35, 36.

CHAPTER VIII.

THE PROMISE OF HIS POWER.

The scriptures tell us of a time when God will pour out his Spirit upon his people, which was to take place in the last days of time, and the last days are those from the time of Christ, and prophecy is rapidly being fulfilled; and the time of the end is near at hand when the Lord will be seen coming in the clouds, declaring that time will be no more, and all will be changed in the "twinkling of an eye" at the last trump.

That which was spoken by the prophet Joel, has come to pass, wherein the Lord said, "I will pour out of my Spirit upon all flesh: and your sons and your daughters shall prophesy, and your young men shall see visions, and your old men shall dream dreams: and on my servants and on my hand maidens will I pour out in those days of my Spirit; and they shall prophesy."—Acts 2: 17, 18.

In the last days also it was foretold that many should depart from the "faith once delivered to the saints," and evil doers would wax worse and worse, and spiritual darkness, wars, and rumors of war, pestilence, famine, etc., reign throughout the land; but in the evening time the church shall receive her primitive power, and shine forth with the glory of God, and rivers of living water shall flow from those who believe on the Son of God; and his people shall be a "peculiar people, zealous of good works." Thank God! that time has already come, and is now here. The great judgment day is near at hand, and the church—his bride—is arrayed in the glory of his power, ready to meet him at his coming.

CHAPTER IX.
THE GIFTS OF HEALING.

It has been a question in the minds of many followers of Jesus Christ, whether or not they have a right to claim any of the special gifts of the Spirit, as spoken of in the twelfth chapter of First Corinthians. Every sanctified child of God possesses all these gifts of the Spirit in a degree, although not as a special gift; but to such an extent as to be able to obey the Word in all things. They have a degree of wisdom, of knowledge, faith, etc., sufficient to live a Christian life, and work for the salvation of souls, and yet may not realize any one of them as a special gift. A person will not go far in the active service of the Lord without feeling the need of some special gift of the Spirit, for a close walk and communion with the Lord will open up avenues of labor and usefulness where one will feel like seeking the greatest glory of God by being fully equipped for his service; will feel like obeying 1 Cor. 12: 31, and "covet earnestly the best gifts," in order to be qualified for the work of the Master.

It must be borne in mind that there is a great responsibility resting upon those unto whom God entrusts these precious gifts. "For unto whomsoever much is given, of him shall be much required." God intends that they be used to his glory, and not abused by a lazy, or faithless servant, and His cause thus put to shame. There are persons who fear to move out upon the promises of God and be fully submissive to his will in all things, for fear God will require some great work of them; require them to take some responsible position in his vineyard. Do you know, such ones are a stumbling block to souls? They are generally persons who have more influence over others than they themselves realize, and their faltering steps get them between God and a multitude of souls. Such ones are often made to realize the weight of Luke 12: 47:—"And that servant, which knew his Lord's will, and prepared not himself, neither did according to His will, shall be beaten with many stripes." "To him that knoweth to do good and doeth it not, to him it is sin."—Jas. 4: 17.

To every minister that God sends forth to preach the Gospel, in the commission is to be found the command to go forth and "preach the Gospel, heal the sick," etc.; but how many there are who are not living up to their privileges; not fulfilling the commission.

The promise was that "these signs shall follow them that believe,"—Mark 16: 17; and among the signs mentioned were, "They shall lay hands on the sick, and they shall recover." Jesus also said, "He that believeth on me, the works that I do shall he do also, and greater works than these shall he do; because I go unto my Father."—Jno. 14: 12. It is the privilege and duty of every minister of the Gospel to possess and exercise the gifts of healing, because that comes with the commission, and they should be qualified at any time to respond to the call in James 5: 14-15. So also should every elder possess the gifts of healing, and whoever will receive and use them to the glory of God. But woe unto them who seek these gifts for self praise or for some selfish motive; or who will shrink from exercising the gifts which God has given them, for they "shall be beaten with many stripes." As the members of our body "have not the same office: so we, being many, are one body in Christ, and every one members one of another, having gifts differing according to the grace that is given to us."—Rom. 12: 4-6. It is not necessary for every one to possess any one of the special gifts, yet God withholds from

OF SOUL AND BODY.

none whom he calls to special work for him, if they can and will use the same to his glory, and will follow so closely in his footsteps as to be trusted with such a treasure from the Lord, and not become puffed up, and thereby take the praise themselves, and lose the grace of God, should he see fit to do some wonderful work through them. As to claiming our rights and privileges on this line, no doubt some of my own experience would be of benefit to some one. Until about the time the Lord called me into his service to publish the Gospel, I was taught that the day of miracles was past, and divine healing forever ceased, and was not practiced after the days of the apostles. But by reading my Bible, I soon learned different, and was not only convinced that the Word taught that I had been falsely instructed, but found that God had a people who believed his word, and practiced its teaching.

Soon after being called into the work of the Lord, I felt the need of some special gifts of the Spirit, and especially the gifts of healing. Not considering myself a preacher, it was a question in my mind as to whether or not I had a right to claim the same. And when convictions came that I ought to possess certain gifts, I would pray over the matter, and ask the Lord to show me his will regarding it. Soon after a young brother and myself attended a cottage prayer meeting where the Lord wonderfully manifested His power. In the same room was a boy of fourteen years of age who had been sick for several weeks, and at the close of the meeting he asked us to lay hands on him and ask the Lord to heal him. Now came the test. Neither of us had ever laid on hands for healing, but we proceeded in the name of the Lord, and the boy was instantly healed. The devil tried to make me believe it was all done through the faith of the young man who was with me, and that I did not possess the gift.

I once more sought the Lord to know his will, and a few days later, while at the house of an elder of the church, a sister who was very much afflicted with a chronic disease—scrofula in her face—desired to obey James 5: 14, and a deep conviction came upon me that I should lay on hands; and about the same time the elder turned to me and invited me to do so, and the sister was instantly healed, and gave God the glory. Knowing that many had been healed through the prayers of this elder, I again permitted the enemy to bring the same accusation. The Lord showed me in different ways that it was my privilege to claim it, so I asked him to give me a chance to test the matter. Not long after, a sister came several miles, with a very sick babe, to get me to lay on hands and pray for its recovery. This time there was no one to lay on hands with me, and I proceeded according to James 5: 14, 15, believing the Lord would raise up the child. Not much change was to be seen as she took her departure for home, and it was a number of days before the child fully recovered. I was still in doubt regarding the gift, when a brother instructed me on this line, and presented the Word of God on the subject, and told me that as God had called me to such a responsible position it was necessary for me to possess the gifts of healing, and I should make a special consecration or request of the Lord, and claim them, which I did, and from that time have not doubted my possession of these favors, and have since seen hundreds of persons healed of various diseases by the power of God, and truly realize that the "prayer of faith" saves the sick, and the Lord does the raising up.

CHAPTER X.
WHO ARE THE ELDERS?

According to the instruction given in James 5: 14, the question would naturally arise, Who are the elders? In every community where God has his church established and set in order, there are one or more elders, or overseers of the flock. And to whom God calls to such a responsible position, he also bestows upon them the gifts of healing, that they may be able to respond to the call spoken of in James. The elder who does not possess these gifts is not living up to his privileges, nor fulfilling his calling, because he is unable to administer to the wants of those under his care.

The qualifications of an elder are to be found in Titus 1: 5-9; 1 Tim. 3: 1-7.

Deacons likewise must have the same moral qualifications as an elder, and it is their duty to look after the needs of the church, and it is almost necessary for them to possess these gifts in order to fulfill their calling. Again, there are others who are not especially called to the office of elder, as overseer, or teacher in the church, who possess the special gifts of healing, and in the absence of the ruling elders or together with them can obey the call in James 5: 14, and Mark 16: 16-18. They must have a special call to this work, the same as one would to the call of the ministry. Even a minister has no right to lay on hands according to James 5: 14, unless he has faith. In case of an emergency, any one who has the faith can lay on hands for healing and the Lord will honor the same.

CHAPTER XI.
WHAT KIND OF OIL TO USE.

Ever since the days of the patriarchs of old, the oil of olive has been used for sacred purposes. It was one of the ingredients used in making the ointment used by Moses for anointing purposes. The Hebrew name for this ointment is *shemen*.

The oil spoken of in James 5: 14; Mark 6: 13; Luke 7: 46, and many other places where used for anointing purposes, means OIL OF OLIVE, and is translated from the Greek word *claion*. Here we find the oil of olive an ointment of itself, used especially for anointing the sick, and for other sacred purposes.

CHAPTER XII.
ANOINTING AND CONSECRATION.

Of the anointing spoken of in the Bible we should not fail to remember that the first one should be the anointing of the soul by the Holy Spirit. The soul should be at peace with God, and abounding in his love, where it will be a pleasure to walk in the footsteps of Jesus, and follow his instructions in all things. Yet how often we find some of his followers lagging just as far behind as they can possibly get, without completely losing sight of the Savior, seemingly afraid to trust in his word, and obey his command. O faithless generation, awake from your drifting state of unbelief; get out of "Doubting Castle," and into the front ranks of battle, on the line of faith, ready to follow the command of him who leadeth on to victory.

Some are willing to do almost anything else, when sick, except obey the instruction in James 5: 14, and send for the elders to anoint them with oil and pray over them. It is no wonder they are chastened of the Lord, and "beaten with many stripes," as it were. There is something very sacred about the anointing with oil. The virtue is not in the oil, and merely rubbing on a little oil of itself would do no good, but it is to be done because the Word of God instructs us to do so, and the anointing is to be done *in the name of the Lord*. We read (Mark 6: 13) that the apostles " anointed with oil many that were sick, and healed them." The Lord has not changed his method of healing, and the same is done to day among his true followers. The child of God who will not take God for a physician for the body as well as for the soul, is a rebellious child, and spends hours of needless suffering. O how sweet to be just where we can trust God for all things.

CHAPTER XIII.
CAN I BE HEALED?

Many who have long been suffering with some chronic or acute disease, the question naturally arises, Can I ever be healed? A few questions in response, may throw some light upon the subject for you. Are you at peace with God, wholly sanctified to do his will, abounding in his love? if not, it is your duty and privilege to be wholly the Lord's. Is God getting any glory out of your sickness? if not, you had better obey and believe his word, and be healed. Have you called for the elders, or had the prayer of faith offered? Have you earnestly enquired of the Lord to know the cause of your sickness? and would you remove the cause if he were to show you your duty on that line? His promises are sure, and if you earnestly seek him, if it is not his will to heal you he will reveal it unto you, and give you grace to bear your affliction.

CHAPTER XIV.
SICK FOR THE GLORY OF GOD.

"Many are the afflictions of the righteous: but the Lord delivereth him out of them all."—Psa. 34: 19. Yet there are many spending a whole life time of pain and misery, unable to work for the Lord or for themselves, wearing away the threads of life, and still keeping up as much courage and patience as possible, trying to make themselves believe it is the will of God for them to thus continue life unto the end, and be "made perfect through suffering." If any one desire, and prefer such a life, amen; let them have it. But the Lord promises us better things. He promises to "take away all our diseases," and in his word sets forth the remedy. The Lord often receives glory through the affliction of his children. Often the souls of others are brought to him through the affliction of some of his children, but it is generally by the manifestation of his power in healing the affliction. He permits afflictions to come upon others sometimes because they disobey some of his laws, and fail to walk uprightly before him as they should; or to bring them to a point where they will make a complete surrender to his will in all things, and their souls receive a fresh anointing from the presence of the Lord to equip them for future service in his vineyard. The parent who loves his child will chasten it when necessary, and continue the same until it becomes obedient. So it is with our heavenly parent; he often sees fit to "chasten whom he loveth," and "scourgeth every son whom he receiveth."—Heb. 12: 6. Dear children of God should not, when afflictions come upon them, feel that God has forsaken them, but on the other hand seek earnestly to know his will, and be obedient. To do otherwise would be rebellion against his will, and bring a more severe chastening.

A few months ago a woman wrote me a letter, and said she had been almost a helpless invalid for over forty years, and felt it was the will of God to patiently endure her sickness, yet she knew of no special way in which he was receiving glory, except through her being made perfect through suffering.

It is through doing the will of God that we are made perfect. Many would become exalted, and turn from the ways of the Lord, were his chastening rod not applied when needed. When will the lesson of obedience be learned, his word believed, and the affliction removed?

It is true Paul had an affliction which he sought the Lord to remove, and received the answer, " My grace is sufficient;" but this affliction did not prevent him working for the Lord, and doubtless kept him humble and true to God. We have no evidence as to whether this " thorn in the flesh " remained or not. It may have been removed shortly after he sought the Lord to take it away. But be that as it may. Paul was consecrated to all the will of God, and went about his " Master's business."

We should be consecrated to suffer just as long as God desires, but there is great need of people being awakened to the great need of more earnestly seeking to know the will of the Lord and act accordingly.

CHAPTER XV.
THE USE OF MEDICINE.

The use of medicine is for two classes of persons, viz: Those who are not acquainted with God, and those of his children who are afraid to trust him. And while there are some medicines which may be used beneficially at times, yet the words of a learned doctor are very true; he said: "If all the medicines on earth were cast into the seas, humanity would be better off, but it would be worse off for the fishes."

No doubt we were once about all of us medicine topers, and for health and strength were leaning upon the "wisdom of men," which is "foolishness to God." But since we have learned to believe the Word of God, and move out upon his promises, it is an easy thing to trust him alone in times of sickness. Some one asks, What about broken bones? In such cases, if no one present were capable of setting it properly, I should call a physician or surgeon, if necessary, to set it, and ask the Lord to heal it. I have known of persons having their limbs broken, and by setting the bones and calling upon the Lord to heal them, in less than three days had full use of the injured limb.

CHAPTER XVI.
MEANS WHICH GOD BLESSES.

People say, "God blesses means, and we should do all we can and ask his blessings upon the same." To be sure there are things which can at times be given to relieve the sick. But there is no remedy so effective as the one given in the Bible for the children of God to use; none so easily applied. But instead of using this God-given remedy, which can be had without money and without price, people will dope themselves with poisonous drugs, pay doctor bills, and thus rob God of means that should be used to his glory. Here! you Christian professors, just stop a moment and estimate the amount you have paid out for medicine and doctor bills for the last five or ten years; then see how much you have paid out for the cause of Christ, and see if God has been receiving his just dues at your hand. Take into consideration the fact that he offers his treatment free. And his prescriptions are for each member of his family; not one excluded. The only thing required is to obey his word. Now let us see if some of us have not been very slack regarding some of our privileges. There is a faithful promise in his word that will meet the case of every one, no difference where they are, or what their trouble or afflictions may be. God blesses means; but the means he intends for his children to use are those set forth in his word. What kind is that? It is PRAYER and FAITH. James says, "Is any sick among you? let him call for the elders of the church; and let them pray over him, anointing him with oil in the name of the Lord: and the prayer of faith shall save the sick; and the Lord shall raise him up."—James 5: 14, 15. Here we see that the work is done through the prayer of faith, and the Lord does the raising up.

But suppose there are no elders in the community? Then we have this promise: That if two of you shall agree on earth as touching anything that they shall ask, it shall be done for them of my Father which is in heaven. For where two or three are gathered together in my name, there am I in the midst of them.—Matt. 18: 19, 20. Sometimes it happens that a person becomes seriously ill, or in great distress, and not even one child of God can be brought to the rescue. Is there a promise in such a case? O yes; a very precious one. Jesus says, "If ye abide in me and my words abide in you, ask what ye will and it shall be done unto you."—Jno. 15: 7. Just emphasize the first part of that promise, and examine yourselves and see if you are abiding in him; for it is only the abiding ones to whom this promise is given. If you are a sinner you have the privilege of repenting of your sins, and then the promise will be yours.

"And this is the confidence we have in him, that if we ask anything according to his will, he heareth us: and if we know that he hear us, whatsoever we ask, we know that we have the petitions that we desired of him."—1 Jno. 5: 14, 15. James says: "Is any among you afflicted? let him pray." The injunction of the scripture is not to flee for a doctor in time of sickness, but rather flee to the Lord, who is the Great Physician; who forgiveth all thine iniquities; who healeth all thy diseases."—Psa. 103: 3. Be assured that if in any case of sickness the doctor can do you any good, the Lord can do much more for you, without the aid of the doctor or his medicine. If you have no faith in God, and want to take medicine, take it. But you will find what little medicine you do take will weaken the small portion of faith which you have, because you look to the medicine for results, and not unto the Lord; and while the taking of medicine may not be a sin of itself, yet it shows a lack of faith and trust in God, and opens broad avenues for the sin of unbelief, and in most cases is the very cause and hindrance of a complete cure being effected.

One excuse is, "I have no faith." Get it then, for faith is a gift of God, and Paul tells us to "covet earnestly the best gifts." This great blessing is given for the asking. Why not possess it? It would seem very foolish for afflicted persons to declare that it was not the will of God to heal them, and yet keep on doctoring and pouring down medicine with a hope of being cured in that way. Yet there are many who are doing that very thing. Why not settle down and be content with your lot, if you believe it is his will for you to suffer, and use your drug money for the good of others? You will find it always more safe to trust your case in the hands of the Lord, than to trust in physicians. May God help his children to consider these things from a Bible standpoint.

CHAPTER XVII.
THE PRAYER OF FAITH.

In considering this subject, let us notice a few of the precious promises of the Lord and see if it is safe to pray the prayer of faith, and leave the results with God. If ye have faith, Jesus says, "Nothing shall be impossible unto you" (Matt. 17: 20); and "If ye abide in me, and my words abide in you, ask what ye will, and it shall be done unto you" (John 15: 17). "If ye shall ask anything in my name, I will do it" (John 14: 15). "And this is the confidence that we have in him, that if we ask anything according to his will, he heareth us: and if we know that he hear us, whatsoever we ask, we know that we have the petitions that we desired of him."— 1 John 14: 15

Now we will review the oft quoted passage in James 5: 13–16. "Is any among you afflicted," what must he do? take medicine? No; "LET HIM PRAY." "Is any sick among you? let him call for the elders of the church; and let them pray over him, anointing him with oil in the name of the Lord: *and the prayer of faith shall save the sick, and the Lord shall raise him up.*" When the prayer of faith is offered, the disease is rebuked, and the case in the hands of the Lord, and he does the raising up. Whether it is done instantly, or a gradual amending, from that time, does not matter; his word stands true, and it is for us to believe and doubt not, trusting him to sweep away the disease in any way he sees fit. But one thing remember, and that is, when you have fully complied with the Word of God, and offered the prayer of faith, from that very moment you can declare yourself healed by the power of God, because his word says, "If we know that he hear us, whatsoever we ask, we know that we have the petitions that we desired of him." Although in some cases the symptoms and even the pain may linger for some time, yea, be increased many times, but faith declares it is done. The tempter whispers, You dare not claim it, you are not healed. But at such times the true believer rests secure in the promises of Jesus, believing, trusting, and giving God the glory, realizing that God is true to his word, and that Satan is not only a liar, but is the father of lies.

It is not necessary to send for the elders for every affliction and disease that may come upon a person, for the instructions to such a one is, " Let him pray." Wait upon the Lord and he will heal your afflictions. If a person is really sick and cannot exercise faith, or has some chronic disease which his faith fails to reach, then let him call for the elders and fully comply with the Word of God.

CHAPTER XVIII.
WALKING OUT UPON HIS PROMISES.

Now we have reached the point where our faith is to be tested; whether or not we are willing to trust the Lord and take him at his word, against all opposition, symptoms, feeling, temptations, etc. We come to genuine faith, that which reaches beyond human vision, and accepts the Word as true, leaving no room for doubt or failure. It is the point where we not only claim that which is our own, but we take possession of that claim.

OF SOUL AND BODY.

Suppose a man were to offer to sell a valuable watch for ten dollars, and you being in great need of one, speedily make the purchase by paying him the ten dollars. From that moment the watch is yours whether you reach out and take it or not. But it does you no good whatever as long as you do not take possession of it. Just so with the blessed treasures to be received from the rich treasure house of the Lord. He offers them upon conditions; we meet the conditions and have full right to the blessing, but it fails to do us any good unless we demand our rights, show our warrant and authority in his word, and take possession of what belongs to us. Shortly after the Lord called me to work for him, I learned a very precious lesson on this line. There was much sickness in the community in which I lived; three of our family had been stricken down with fever, and passed through a severe siege of sickness. I soon felt the disease taking hold upon me, but withstood it for several days, but was finally overpowered by the disease, and after lying in bed a few hours with a burning fever, and suffering the most excruciating pain, I began to earnestly commune with the Lord; and told him that he had called me to work that in my present condition I was unable to do. As there were no elders present upon whom I could call, I began to refer the Lord to many of his wonderful promises, among which was John 15: 7, "If ye abide in me and my words abide in you, ask what ye will and it shall be done unto you." I searched my consecration, and asked the Lord to search me. I was willing to suffer if it was his will, but I longed to be about my "Master's business." I said, "Lord, I am abiding in thee and thy word abides in me, so the promise is mine. I give my case fully into thy hands, and I pray thee to heal me." Then I waited for the work to be done, but no change came. Finally I said, "Lord, why am I not healed?" The answer seemed to come at once: "Take the Lord at his word and arise." I said, "Amen, Lord, I will." And without hesitating a moment I began to get out of bed. It seemed as if my head would burst with pain, and in my weakness I began to dress myself. When half dressed a slight change came over me, and dropping upon my knees I thanked the Lord for it. After dressing and rendering thanks again I was much better, and walked into another room declaring that the Lord had healed me Within twenty minutes the fever had entirely left me, and I immediately went to work, and was well from that hour. I am confident had I lain there and not moved out upon naked faith, I would have had to pass through a long siege of sickness. To God be all the praise. It taught me a very valuable lesson of trusting him, and moving out upon his promises, the remembrance of which has been of great benefit to me, and I tell of it only for the glory of God, hoping that others may be benefited by the same.

CHAPTER XIX.
RESISTING TEMPTATION.

After having stepped out upon the promises of the Lord and taken him for our physician, it is then the business of the devil to throw out his temptations in in every way possible. If he cannot make us doubt our healing he will sometimes offer to help the matter along a little by some of his suggestions. And then try to accuse and condemn the one who listens to and follows his advice. The Word says, " Resist the devil and he will flee from you."—James 4: 7. When the tempter comes we will find it an easy matter to resist him if we take into consideration the wonderful promises of God, and that he promises to deliver us out of the hands of the enemy at all times, and all we have to do is to trust Him and do his bidding, " Blessed is the man that endureth temptation: for when he is tried he shall receive the crown of life which the Lord hath promised to them that love him."—James 1: 12. " There hath no temptation taken you but such as is common to man: but God is faithful who will not suffer you to be tempted above that ye are able; but will with the temptation also make a way to escape, that ye may be able to bear it."—1 Cor. 10: 13.

CHAPTER XX.
RESISTING THE TRUTH.

People often bring afflictions upon themselves through disobeying the laws of nature, but there are times when God in his wisdom sees fit to send his judgments upon rebellious persons such as resist the truth and bitterly persecute his children. Such was the case with those who came up against the prophet Elisha(2 Kings 6: 18), and they were smitten with blindness.

Saul was smitten with blindness while he was breathing out threatenings against the saints of God. (Acts 9: 1-9.)

Elymas the sorcerer received the same fate, and was blind for a season because he withstood Paul and Barnabas.

A few years ago a man in Southern Indiana had for some time been bitterly opposing God's true and faithful children, and one afternoon was suddenly smitten with blindness, and is yet in that condition.

Such is the fate of many who resist the truth of God, and persecute his faithful followers. All are not smitten with blindness, but are in other ways made to realize that the Lord is God, and that he is not to be mocked, and his truth resisted, without bringing a penalty upon the persecutors.

CHAPTER XXI.
HINDRANCES TO HEALING.

In seeking the Lord for the blessing of health, it is well to consider a few points, and first know whether or not it is his will to heal us, and see if we are consecrated to suffer just as long as he in his wisdom sees fit to permit us to be afflicted. When once satisfied that it is his will to restore us to health, find out when he promises to do it. Seek to know the cause, and remove the same, as far as lieth in your power. James says, "Confess your faults," etc., that ye may be healed. O how often people fail to be healed just because they do not follow this instruction; and by trying to cover up, and hide that which should be confessed, they fail to receive the desired blessing. It is when the Word is complied with that the Lord has promised to forgive the sins which have been the means of bringing on the disease. There are numberless obstacles in the way of healing, which may all be summed up in a few words and the matter settled at once. First, find out the cause, if possible, and if caused by any wrong on your part, forsake the wrong, confess the same to God, and if necessary to his children, then the prayer of faith can be offered with all confidence, knowing that he will grant the request. We are healed for the glory of God, and not to consume our strength upon the lusts of the flesh. Men sometimes apply for healing of dyspepsia, etc. caused by the use of tobacco, expecting to continue the filthy habit. Women suffering from some dreadful trouble brought on by lacing and wearing of corsets, too often desire to be healed but are not willing to remove the cause. Persons practicing filthy habits, abusers of themselves, etc., call on God to heal them and yet will not turn from that which makes themselves self-murderers. Is it any wonder that the world says faith healing is a failure?

When people get in line with God just where he desires them to be, they will either be healed or God will receive glory through their sickness, and enable them to rejoice through it all, with the comforting words, " My grace is sufficient."

CHAPTER XXII.
CASTING OUT DEVILS.

We read in the Bible that Christ and his apostles went about healing the sick, casting out devils, etc., and in the last chapter of St. Mark he gives the same

OF SOUL AND BODY.

commission and power to "them that believe" upon his word.

Some are really astonished to learn that devils are cast out in these days. It is no uncommon thing for God's true ministers to meet with persons who are possessed with evil spirits, and cast them out. We have witnessed cases doubtless as bad as any spoken of in the Bible, and been present when the devils were cast out. In one case the victim seemed to be possessed with legions of devils, but in answer to prayer and faith was delivered and set free before a public audience, and of the many sinners who witnessed the scene none could gainsay it. Some time ago a brother and myself were called upon to pray for a girl who had been having spasms very frequently for some time. As soon as she saw us coming she declared she would not allow us to pray for her, and as we entered the house she ran from room to room despite her parents' admonitions, refusing to talk or be talked to. We at once saw that it was a clear case of devils, and while she was in an adjoining room we knelt in prayer and rebuked the devil and commanded him to depart. As we arose from our knees she seemed like a different girl, and the devils having been cast out she desired us to pray for the healing of her body. Of the great number of people who are now in the insane asylums, doubtless, most of them are possessed with devils, and were the devils cast out, such persons would be well and clothed in their right mind.

CHAPTER XXIII.
SENDING ANOINTED HANDKERCHIEFS.

It sometimes happens that some of God's true children become sick and feel it their duty to call upon the elders and be anointed for healing, but on account of living a great distance from any of the elders they are unable to send and have them come. In such cases where there is a special leading in that direction, it is pleasing to the Lord for them to send for an anointed handkerchief.

In Acts 19: 12 we read that " God wrought special miracles by the hands of Paul: so that from his body were brought unto the sick handkerchiefs or aprons, and the diseases departed from them, and the evil spirits went out of them."

Before sending for or sending a handkerchief, persons should positively know that they are being led by the Spirit of the Lord in the matter.

Some time ago a sister in New York after a few weeks' severe sickness sent for an anointed handkerchief, and upon receipt of it had it applied in the name of Jesus, and she was enabled at once to arise from her bed and walk about the room praising God for

OF SOUL AND BODY.

his wonderful healing power. A sister in California was healed of cancer in the same way. We could relate a number of cases of wonderful healing in this way, but it is unnecessary to speak of it here. We frequently receive requests to send a handkerchief, and for various reasons do not feel led to send one. A person must have the proper faith, and not merely try an experiment, because it is a work for God, and is not to be trifled with by doubting Thomas's and skeptics. In cases of sickness where persons are thus isolated from the children of God, it is well to send to those who are strong in faith, requesting their special prayers at an appointed time, and God will honor the "prayer of faith" according to James 5: 16; Matt. 18: 19; Jno. 15: 7; 1 Jno. 5: 14, 15. Once a telegram came desiring us to pray immediately for a woman who was violently insane. All work was stopped and as we gathered together for prayer, and laid the case before the Lord, in a few minutes the message came from heaven that the work was done, and the room seemed filled with the glory of God. We believed without a doubt that she was delivered from her insanity; and as soon as the next mail arrived from that place, we received a letter stating that she was instantly delivered and healed.

One night at the midnight hour a loud rap was heard at our door, and the messenger was a boy, who had come with all possible haste, and asked us to pray at once for his father who was dying. We arose from our bed and earnestly called upon the Lord; and rebuked the disease in the name of Jesus; and when the boy reached home again he found his father was healed of his disease and able to be up, and in a few days was perfectly well.

These things are mentioned in this chapter only for the glory of God, and that his children may be strengthened in faith.

CHAPTER XXIV.
SPIRITUALISM.

One of the most deceptive and sure ways of leading souls to destruction and everlasting torment is that of spiritualism. On account of "the working of Satan with all power and signs and lying wonders," often under the pretense or garb of Christianity, spiritualism has been the means of leading many honest souls down to everlasting ruin. Some through curiosity, others for the purpose of knowing some hidden mysteries, enter the circle and witness the performance of "the spirits," who are "called up," and cause the tables, chairs, etc. to dance about the room; who tell something about some departed friend, or something of the kind, just enough to deceive souls who are

OF SOUL AND BODY.

simple enough, or through ignorance of the great danger, tamper with such works of the devil.

The Word of God tells us that Satan can transform himself into an angel of light in order to better practice his deceptions. These spirits which they claim to call up are not by any means the spirits of some departed friends, but it is only the devil as an "angel of light," come to delude and deceive souls. Satan has power to "perform wonders in the sight of men," and under the name of spiritualism people are sometimes healed of various diseases by the power of the devil. But O how appalling the consequences! As a general thing the one healed becomes a believer in spiritualism, a disbeliever in Christ, and often possessed with evil spirits. To become a spiritualistic medium is to sell your soul to the devil, become possessed with evil spirits, deny the saving power of Christ through his precious blood, deny the existence of a devil, or that there is such a place as hell. God deliver souls from such deceptions; from spiritualism and all its soul-deceiving ways! Let a person filled with the Holy Spirit go into their midst and rebuke the devil and all the powers of darkness in the name of Jesus and they are powerless. The "departed spirits," as they call them, will not answer nor perform. Praise God! He has given us power over all devils and spirits of devils to cast them out.

Blessed be his name forever! In the name of Jesus we warn every one to have no part nor lot in the belief or performances of spiritualism if you value your soul. And to those who are already in its clutches we would say, For your souls' sake renounce the deceptions of the devil, call upon God, and he will deliver you out of the snare of the enemy, and give you continual joy and peace to your souls.

CHAPTER XXV.
CHRISTIAN SCIENCE.

Another one of the snares of the enemy of souls is that of Christian Science. It teaches that "sin is not forgiven; we cannot escape its penalty."—11, 165. The Bible says, "If we confess our sins he is faithful and just to forgive us our sins."—1 Jno. 1: 9.

"Science decides matter or the mortal body to be nothing but a belief and an illusion."—11, 193. Paul refutes such teaching in these words, " Let not sin therefore reign in your mortal body."—Rom. 6: 12. "He shall also quicken your mortal bodies by His Spirit that dwelleth in you."—Rom. 8: 2.

These are only a few of the many direct contradictions between Christian Science and the Bible. Yet they make the healing of the body one of their specialities, but do not do it in the name of Jesus, nor according to the Bible. Honest people often go to

OF SOUL AND BODY. 131

them for treatment and leave with a shattered mind and a blighted soul. The mind cure, hypnotism, mesmerism, electric power, etc. are other modes of cure which the devil makes use of to show his " signs and wonders," but are none of them used or needed in divine healing. The Lord speaks the word and the work is done, and all we have to do is to obey his word, fully trusting in his promises. It does not cost a person anything to know the secret of divine healing, because the whole thing is to be found in his word; neither does it cost anything to be healed, for the promise is, Believe and ye shall receive.

CHAPTER XXVI.
WITNESSES SINCE THE APOSTLES.

Noted and reliable historians and writers inform us of so many cases of divine healing, and miracles being wrought since the days of the apostles that it is unnecessary to give space in this volume for testimonies of what has taken place during the past centuries. But for the benefit of those wishing to further investigate the subject we would refer you to a few of the noted writers; such as Justin Martyr, Tertullian, Irenacus, Origen, Clement, Milner, Mosheim; in whose works will be found proof that the time of miracles extended down through the different centuries, and did not cease at the death of the apostles; verifying the words of Jesus: " He that believeth on me, the works that I do shall he do also," giving no limit of time, and making no provisions for a time to come when he would not fulfill his word. Among those whose fame has become world-wide, on account of her power with God, and healing the sick through prayer and faith, is Dorothea Trudel, who was born near the beginning of the nineteenth century, and lived in Zurich, Switzerland. She was of humble birth, and passed through many privations in life, and as she advanced in years her faith became so strong in the Lord, that she ventured to lay hands on the sick and ask Him to heal them, and He honored her faith and raised them up. In a short time her house was thronged with sick folks, and as many were healed, the medical profession was stirred because they were losing customers. She was arrested for treating the sick without license, and was fined, and ordered to dismiss her patients. As they were dismissed, her house was at once filled with others. She testified that she used no medicines and prevented no one from using medicines; that she knew nothing about diseases, but only knew that her Savior could heal every sickness.

She appealed to a higher court, which decided that there was no law to prevent any one from praying and laying on hands for the healing of the sick;

OF SOUL AND BODY. 133

so she was acquitted, and her accusers had all the costs to pay. During the trial many persons testified in favor of divine healing, and instead of the doctors putting a stop to the work, it spread a hundred fold more, and people came flocking from every direction to find out something about the dealings of the Lord with his people. Since that time a number of faith homes have been established, both in this country and in foreign lands.

There are people here in the United States who are just about as foolish as the doctors of Switzerland were, who threaten to arrest any one who sees fit to trust themselves in the hands of God, instead of the hands of doctors. Yet not one of the doctors will insure a cure. Let them threaten! there is no law that requires a person to apply to any certain physician; and if any should see fit to apply to the Great Physician for healing, let them do so, despite the threatenings of all opposers; and if any one is sent to jail, God will receive the glory.

When a person moves out upon the promises of God in obedience to his will, earnestly contending for the faith once delivered unto the saints, a work will be wrought which will result in delivering souls out of the hands of the enemy. Satan will be stirred, and foam out his wrath through his children, but God puts a wall of salvation about those who put their trust in him, which is a perfect protection from all the powers of the evil one; "For He shall give His angels charge over thee, to keep thee in all thy ways."

No one follows in the footsteps of Jesus without passing through the fire of persecution. Many times God sees fit to permit sore afflictions to come upon persons in order to teach them lessons of obedience. But he has promised to deliver his children out of them all. To Him be all the praise and glory. Amen.

WITNESSES OF TO-DAY.

PART III.

A WONDERFUL DELIVERANCE.

FOR the benefit of suffering humanity, I will give my experience in regard to divine healing of the body, in connection with my experience of salvation, hoping to point others to Jesus, our life and our saving health among all nations.

I was born Aug. 23, 1853, in the state of Iowa. Three years later my parents settled in the state of Missouri, in the county of Pettis, two miles north-east of Windsor, where I remained until I was twenty-seven years of age. My years were almost an unbroken chain of suffering. Myself and God alone knew the extent of my afflictions, which began in my childhood.

I had spasms from the time I was six years of age, also dyspepsia set in near the same time, and in all my travels I have not witnessed a more severe case.

In a few years spinal affection added much pain to my afflicted body, and with many other diseases and weaknesses, was confined to my bed for months, at different times. All this combined with a stammering tongue, made my life miserable.

I was never able to do any hard work, not even a washing for myself, and the physicians gave me no promise of future health. Many times I would weep and lament, and wonder why God had ever permitted me to live. My dear, good Christian mother would try to cheer me, and tell me that we should not question the ways of the Almighty, and that God had a bright design in all this. But that was a mystery which God alone could solve, and it failed to remove the sadness or the pain.

All was dark, so dark to me, for I could not look out in the future with one bright hope. But in my nineteenth year, May 3, 1872, having repented of my sins, I received Jesus as my Savior, and his Spirit bore witness with my spirit, that I was a child of God. On the fourth day of the following month, I made a complete consecration for time and eternity, and was sanctified wholly. Since then I have been "perfecting in holiness," "growing in grace."

Having been taught that the time of healing was past, I did not seek for it, but came to the conclusion that I was to be made perfect through suffering, as I knew of no one who had ever been healed, until the spring of 1880. My oldest brother being greatly afflicted with chronic diseases, was healed in answer to prayer, without medicine, just by faith in the promises of the Word of God. I could not doubt it, but thought it was not for me. After some months God showed me that I had faith to be healed, and that I was responsible, and if I put in the rest of my life suffering, I did it by choice, and at the risk of my soul. I pondered over this matter for some days. On waking one morning I said to myself, "I am going to let the Lord heal me to day if he will." Then the enemy whispered, You should put it off a week or two, as you have not quite enough faith yet to be healed, and by that time your faith will be strong.

Next came the voice of Jesus, saying, "Oh! thou of little faith, wherefore didst thou doubt?" Then dropping on my knees, I cried: Lord, if it is unbelief, take it out, root and branch; and I knew he did. Then I said, Lord, what next? And he showed me that I should pour out my medicine. I did not know why. Then God revealed to me that I was going to be severely tempted, and if I had the medicine I would be sure to take it, and lose faith for healing. So I poured out the medicine. God showed me that if I was to doubt his word that says, "Who healeth all thy diseases," "The prayer of faith shall save the sick," etc., I would not stop until I would reject it all; would die an infidel; be lost in hell, and be the means of scores of others being lost. I said to Mother, "If you ever prayed earnestly for me, pray for me now." So we bowed together in prayer. After she prayed, I began praying, and claimed the promise in Matt. 18: 19. I said, Lord, thou hast said: That if two shall agree on earth as touching anything that they shall ask, it shall be done unto them of my Father which is in heaven. Now, Lord, we are agreed that thou heal me, soul, body and mind, as complete as is most to thy glory. And as I said it I laid hold on the healing power, and the witness came from heaven that the work was done. I arose from my knees, saying, Mother, it is done; I am healed. I felt the virtue go through my body, and oh, the showers of heavenly grace that filled my soul! I began to praise the Lord, and shouted, giving God the glory. Oh, it was so heavenly. "My soul was joyful in glory," for glory filled my soul. Then was fulfilled that which was spoken by the prophet Isaiah, saying: "Then shall the lame man leap as a hart, and the tongue of the dumb sing: for in the wilderness shall waters break out, and streams in the desert."– Isa. 35: 6.

This was the beginning of a new era in my life. And I remarked that it was the beginning of months to me, as it was the first time in all my recollection that I could say I was well. It was the first bright hope of health that I ever had in this world. The same day I could eat and drink anything that was fit for a sound stomach, without the slightest injury, which I could never do before.

That night the trial came. It seemed that all hell was let loose to try to beat me out of my healing faith, and bring back all my old chronic diseases. Had I not poured out my medicine, surely I would have yielded; but I clung to the promises of God, and rebuked the devil until nearly morning; so God fulfilled this promise, "Resist the devil. and he will flee from you." Then there was a great calm. It seemed almost like angels came and ministered unto me. "My joy was full; my cup ran over." My faith was strong and steady; my appetite good. I walked the floor for several days, with almost ceaseless praises going up to God.

It was circulated through the neighborhood that "Mary Cole was having a whole camp-meeting by herself. She claimed that God had healed her, but it was only excitement, and as soon as the excitement was over she would be as bad off as ever."

My strength increased rapidly and I soon went to a protracted meeting held by the M. E's, as I was then a member of that sect. When opportunity was given for testimonies, I arose and told of God's wonderful dealing with me; how he had pardoned all my sins; made me his child, and afterwards sanctified me wholly; and had so recently healed my poor afflicted body. And I exhorted the people to get rid of their unbelief, and to move out for God on the Bible line. But the preacher came to talk to me about the matter, and said he did not doubt me being healed, but I must not testify to it, for it was too much light for the people, and I must keep still about it, etc.

I then concluded that I would not testify any more to my healing. From that moment the floodgate of hell was open. Gross darkness was upon me. The powers of hell were fast gathering to destroy both soul and body; my mind was almost reeling; intense suffering began in my body. O it was indescribable! God showed me that I had broken my contract to please the blinded sect preacher; and that I must renew my contract with God, and resist the devil, obey God in all things and all would be well. So I did, and my soul was at liberty. My faith was again unwavering, and my strength increasing. A large scrofulous ulcer on my face was

OF SOUL AND BODY. 141

soon gone; my blood pure, and such warmth in my system, I had never felt before. It did not require one-half as much cover as usual to keep me warm.

I stammer some yet, but nothing to what I did before I was healed. God made me to understand a few years before, that in the future I must go and preach his gospel. This was again made plain to me when I was healed on the fifteenth day of November, 1880.

He did not show me that I was to go yet; but to search and study the Bible. It was wonderful how the Holy Spirit did teach me, and open up my understanding to comprehend the Word of God.

In the spring of 1882 the way was open for me to go out and work in the vineyard of the Lord, and he showed me that I must go. I could go and be saved, or stay and be lost. I was still a Methodist. They did not license a woman to preach. But the sect preachers found that God could use me in the salvation of souls, and that I was not specially interested in building up any certain sect; so I had an abundance of calls. Sometimes I would preach twice a day during the week, and three times on Sunday, and also attend the altar services. God always gave me sufficient strength. After a few years all sectarian scales fell from my eyes. I asserted my liberty and have been preaching the pure Gospel on the New Testament line.

I have had a few sick brashes since I was first healed. But God has healed me every time without resorting to doctors or medicine. I am well, soul and body, and can do washings, or hard work of any kind that God requires of me. I recommend my Savior as a Physician for soul and body.

MARY COLE.

Windsor, Mo.

THE BLIND EYES OPENED.

With praise and thanksgiving to God Almighty, I write the following: I had been an invalid for nearly three years. My eyes soon became so weak and sensitive to the light that I was helpless, and had to be led about wherever I went. I had not read a line in three years, lacking one month.

Nine months previous to my healing I was converted to God. Two days after my conversion I was forcibly impressed that I would be healed. I did not know when or where, but I knew the work would be done.

In the month of June, 1883, I received an invitation to attend the annual camp-meeting at Bangor, Mich. I went to my room and inquired earnestly of the Lord if it was his will for me to go, and if that was the place where he would be pleased to heal me. Suddenly a brilliant light, like a flame of fire, encircled me, and the Lord assured me that I would be healed at that meeting. I told my friends what the Lord had showed me, and on making ready to go, requested them to provide me with paper and envelopes, telling them that when healed I would write to them.

Continued prayer was offered in my behalf, and the laying on of hands. On the fourth morn of the meeting I was impressed that I would be healed that day. The same illumination was repeated, and I was filled with the glory of God. Heavenly breezes passed over me from time to time, until about five o'clock in the afternoon while seated with the congregation, on the platform where I had been requested to sit so that all might see, suddenly my eyes opened, and I gazed upon the audience, praising the Lord, to whom be glory forevermore. The people stood in amazement, some shouting, some trembling and crying. Many believed unto salvation when they saw the miracle. The loud shouts of the saints were heard over two miles.

After we had praised God for an hour or more, I went out into the bright sunlight without any unpleasant sensation, the first time for nearly three years; also wrote two postals. Glory to God forever and ever!

My eyes were very much inflamed and granulated, but when the work was done the inflamed and granulated condition left them, and they cleared away perfectly natural. They are bright and strong. I enjoy the unlimited use of them each day. I acknowledge the hand of a wise providence in my affliction, and thank God for it, for by this means he brought me unto himself.

Before I was afflicted I was one of the most worldly, but now I am wholly absorbed in divine things. Jesus is all and in all to me. It is like another world, both spiritually and physically. Glory to His name forever and ever! I will praise Him while I live.

About one year afterward my faith was severely tested. Within a short time my eyelids became badly inflamed, and were very weak and sensitive, getting worse each day. I did not know what to do. While in this condition, a sister who had passed through a similar experience, came to see me, and soon assured me that it was only a trial of my faith. We knelt together in prayer and asked the Lord to give me faith and strength to endure the trial, and when I had been tested sufficiently, to remove every symptom of disease. We claimed perfect victory, and I at once began my usual labor, and resumed my reading, which I had laid by for three days. As I ventured upon God and his promises, new strength was given, and my eyes were fully restored in every respect. I have had similar experiences in other forms of affliction, and have always found him faithful to his word.

From a sister saved and kept by power divine.

EMMA MILLER.

Battle Creek, Mich.

NINE YEARS AN INVALID.

TO ALL THE DEAR READERS AND THE AFFLICTED: May God wonderfully bless and comfort you as you read some of his dealings with me. I cannot enumerate them all with pen and ink, but will attempt to give some truths as they have been manifested unto me for both soul and body.

I was converted when sixteen years of age, and was married at the age of seventeen, in the year 1873. In February, 1874, I was taken sick, and from that time was a helpless invalid until July 18, 1883.

When I was married I felt it my duty to have family worship, but as my husband was not a Christian, I was timid, and put it off, thinking I should do so soon. But the burden kept growing heavier, for I realized the great importance of obeying every leading of the Spirit, but I knew but very little about how to make a real consecration of all things to God at that time.

As I continued to suffer and grow weak, I thought much about the future, and the importance of being prepared to meet the blessed Lord who had suffered so much for one so unworthy as myself. Sometimes preachers would come to visit me, and I would hope that they would say something to give me light, as my poor soul was hungering after something, and I knew not what to ask for, nor how to obtain it. None of them gave me any help in that direction.

In the spring of 1881 my husband thought he would take me to the Eureka Springs of Arkansas, to see if the water would do me any good, as he being a physician, had done all he and other physicians thought would be of any benefit to me. The waters, however, gave me no permanent relief. I felt a little better for a short time but soon became weaker than ever before, insomuch that for six months at a time I was blind; and also lost my voice, and for some length of time was unable to speak above a whisper. But, oh, the glorious light that had begun to spring up in my soul during this time of seeking relief for the body at the Springs!

The dear Lord sent those to me who taught me that there was deliverance for the captives, and how to set the prisoners free; and that it was my privilege to be made whole both soul and body. They showed me by the Word of God that consecration by

OF SOUL AND BODY. 147

faith in Jesus, would bring about sanctification of the soul, and his cleansing blood would destroy the carnal mind which is enmity against God. See Rom. 8: 7, and also the scripture which teaches us to trust God for the healing of the body. I had been taught that the day of healing was past; but when I would read the scripture, and see that God is no respecter of persons; and that he is "the same yesterday, to day, and forever;" also how Jesus used to heal all who came unto him, I believed that he loved his people as much now as when he was here upon earth. But before I was healed my consecration had to reach the point where I was willing to do anything the Lord would have me do, and I was blessed in talking of the goodness of Jesus to every one who came to see me. Oh! the bliss and constant peace of my soul was more than I can find words to express. Instead of the longings, and doubts and fears, there was a sweet communion which words fail to explain, but those who have found "The honey in the Rock," understand my meaning.

I often lay for several days at a time in a cold, prostrate condition, and almost a death-like perspiration upon my body and limbs, so cold that they could not be warmed by friction or stimulants.

I felt a great desire to be baptized, and as I had learned to look to Jesus to be guided by him in all things, this scripture kept coming to my mind: Except ye be born of water, and of the Spirit, ye cannot enter into the kingdom of God.—Jno. 3: 5.

I felt led to have a holiness preacher to baptize me, but I was too weak to be taken out of my room; so they brought a bath-tub into my room, and I was baptized in it. Then I felt so anxious to partake of the Lord's supper, and the same preacher, with a few other Christians came and we had a glorious time commemorating the death of our dear Savior.

We were living in Thayer, Kan., at the time of my healing. A little girl was feeding me my breakfast, and as I was taking some grape-juice and bread, the words of 1 Cor. 11: 25, came to me, and I said: If thy will, accept it as in remembrance of thee, it shall be; and oh! such a witness of His holy presence came with such power. I realized the healing power was present to heal me. I said, The Lord has healed me! and I began to sing " It is done," and then said, What shall I do? The Spirit of the Lord said, Leap and rejoice. And again, Arise and walk. I told the little girl, who had been feeding me, to tell my husband to come in. When he came, I said, Doctor, I am healed; will you believe it? Let me up so I can walk. In the name and strength of Jesus I arose, but cannot describe the change; it was as if I had been carrying all I could possibly live under, and the load suddenly removed. The change was so great, and made me so light and free, that I felt just like running all over town.

The day before I was healed I heard the noise of wings over me. This was repeated three times, and I did not understand what it meant, but as I was so near death's door, supposed that the Lord had sent for me. Shortly after I was healed I was one day reading my Bible, and read Malachi 4: 2: "But unto you that fear my name shall the Sun of righteousness arise with healing in his wings." This explained matters and made it all plain to me.

After being healed, I felt impressed that in order to keep victory for my healing, I should have family worship three times a day; and thus let my light shine for the glory of God. I have since given birth to two children, and each time got up in as good health as before.

With much love and sympathy to all the afflicted, I am resting upon the Solid Rock.

MARY J. SWEENEY.

CORROBORATING TESTIMONY.

In regard to what my wife has written, I can say what she has stated are facts. She had been sick about six years before I took her to the Eureka Springs of Arkansas, with the hope that she would recover her health.

Her disease was a female trouble. She had antifluction and antiversion of the uterus, also mitritus, with ulcers at the os of the worst character. During the six years she was scarcely able at any time to be on her feet, or walk a step.

I had a large practice at that time, but gave her all the attention I could. I perused several of the best works on Jinecology, such as West, Thomas, Monday and others, and consulted some of the best physicians, but we could not reach her case.

We remained at the Springs, with no benefit from the water. We then came back to Thayer, Kan. and remained ten months until my wife was healed. During the ten months she seemed more prostrated than before. She was weak, debilitated and nervous, with quick intermitting pulse, cold perspiration, loss of vision to a great extent, and could not speak louder than a low whisper.

At the time she was healed I was sitting in an adjoining room writing. When she sent for me to come into the room, as I entered I was utterly astonished, and most agreeably surprised when I found her sitting up in the bed. She reached out her hand and said, " Doctor, I am healed, I feel like I could walk all over town." She arose without assistance, and walked to a rocking chair in the room and sat down, rejoicing and praising the Lord. I frankly confess, after witnessing the long, protracted complicated case, and then see her get right up in the midst of it, though an unsaved man, I was afraid to deny the healing power of God.

Dr. R. E. Sweeney.

Chanute, Kan., *July 29, 1891.*

PHYSICIANS BAFFLED FOR ELEVEN YEARS.

Feeling that it would glorify God for me to write my testimony of healing, I willingly obey the leadings of his Spirit. I was bodily afflicted with female weakness which baffled the skill of physicians for over eleven years. I suffered a great deal at times and had to lie on my face for ease. The suffering which I was compelled to endure no one can ever know, except those who pass through the same. It seemed as if I was doomed to live a miserable life the remainder of my days.

The saints came here and preached the everlasting gospel. I accepted the light and was sanctified wholly. At first I was not willing to call for the elders and have them lay hands upon me, but thought I could pray and be healed myself, but God did not answer. I began to think I must go to some physician, yet I hated the thought of doctoring. A dear brother was here holding meeting, and I sent for him, and obeyed James 5: 14, and was healed through and through. O praise the Lord! I am completely healed, and can do my work and help my husband do his.

I afterwards had the measles which seemed to settle on my lungs, leaving symptoms of serious lung trouble; but glory to his name! he has healed me of it all, and I am sound and well. I can never thank the Lord enough for what he has done for me.

Your sister, sanctified to do the whole will of God.

ALICE M. EBERLINE.

DELIVERANCE FROM DISOBEDIENCE.

DEAR ONES IN CHRIST: I feel led to write and tell of the wonderful healing of my body wrought by the omnipotent power of God, according to James 5: 13-15.

Four years ago I was gloriously saved, and God called me to preach his word. I could not see why he should call such a poor, ignorant creature as I, and so I tried to believe that there was a mistake somewhere, and that I was not the one he wanted. But God made me to understand that it was him who had spoken to me, and that I had to preach the gospel or perish. But I refused to obey God, and lost my salvation.

Previous to this time I was a stout, hearty young man, but when I disobeyed the Lord he permitted disease to come upon me, and I was brought very low with consumption and hemorrhage of the lungs. I bled very frequently. So I thought I would rather die and get out of my misery. Ofttimes I would stretch myself upon my bed of sickness, fold my arms and ask God to let me die. But God would not let me go. I tried the different doctors and received some relief, but when I stopped taking their stimulants I was worse than ever. God still followed me, and I could hear him whisper, "You disobeyed me." O what torment I was in! I sought for relief in the foolish things of the world, but I could hear his voice there. I then joined the Ohio National Guards, but he followed me there, and my afflictions still increased, and the people said I was fast dying with consumption. I still thought I would seek death, and wished I could join the Standing Army, where I would have a chance to get shot down, and thereby get rid of all my troubles; but God had his eye upon me, and all my afflictions were becoming still greater. I started and got as far as Sidney, O. The saints were holding a grove meeting at that place, but I was determined not to attend, but was finally persuaded to go, and did so; thank the Lord! He so wonderfully convicted me that I could no longer resist his loving Spirit, and as I yielded to his call he saved my soul.

This was in the year 1889, and I began to work for

the Lord, though my afflictions were very great, but God wonderfully helped me. In the spring of 1890 I went in company with my brother to Hayden, Ind., where I had a very severe attack of bleeding of the lungs, and was unable to attend the meeting. The friends with whom I was staying thought my time in this world was of short duration. I received strength to get to the home of my brother at Sidney, O., and there a relapse took place, and my suffering increased until I was compelled to keep my bed for some time. While suffering there my soul was stirred insomuch that I cried out unto the Lord, and promised him that if he would just raise me up out of my bed I would not shun to declare his word to the people. He answered my prayer. We had a meeting at our house; although I was so weak that I had to hold to the stand to keep from falling while I spoke to the people, and God wonderfully helped me, yet I thought I could not be healed because I had brought my sufferings upon myself by my disobedience, and for that reason would have to suffer it as a thorn in the flesh.

When I came to the camp-meeting at Bangor, Mich., I found that it was the will of God to heal me, and not his will that I should suffer any longer. So I obeyed the Word in James 5: 13-15, and God by his healing power touched my body, and I was made whole from that very hour. O wonderful physician I have found in Jesus!

I am now healed soul and body, and when it is necessary I can do as good a day's work in the harvest field as almost any man. I can truthfully testify to the glory of God that I have as good health as I ever had, and have salvation in addition to it. To sum up the whole matter, I am perfect, entire, wanting nothing; justified, sanctified and HEALED by the power of God.

Yours and Christs,

GEO. W. HOWARD.

Sidney, O., *Aug. 27, 1891.*

HEALED, SOUL, BODY, AND EYES.

DEAR SAINTS AND LOVERS OF THE TRUTH: My heart is full of the love of God, and gratitude to my Savior for his wonderful saving, healing and keeping power. O it is so blessed and glorious to be saved of God, and saved from everything but God. And just as wonderful to be kept. For if we do not keep saved our having been saved will profit us nothing. Truly I have much for which to praise God. Seven years ago last June I attended the camp-meeting of the saints of God near Bangor, Mich. I went there with a sin-sick soul and a body wrecked with disease, and praise God! I returned home saved and sound.

About ten years previous to that time my eyes began troubling me. The lids became granulated and inflamed. I was dress-making at that time. In order to spare my eyes for sewing I would refrain from reading, but growing worse, in about two years I was obliged to give up both. I did therefore, work for about two years, then having taken a cold that settled in my eyes and my whole body, it left my eyes so bad that I was compelled to keep them closed most of the time. From that time I was unable to work. I could walk about some, and use my eyes in a general way, but not to look steadily at anything. About three years later it was discovered that my afflictions were caused by internal organic displacement. I began receiving treatment from one of the prominent physicians of Battle Creek, Mich., where I then lived After the third treatment I was unable to walk, and in a short time my arms became helpless. I was unable to comb my hair, or prepare the victuals on my plate, and so weak I could scarcely drag myself about the house.

While in this wretched condition, my cousin, Emma Miller, was wonderfully healed of God at the Bangor camp-meeting. The same fall, her sister, Mrs. Courtney, was healed at the same place. I was too weak to attend that meeting, it being about sixty miles from my home. The next June was the time

OF SOUL AND BODY.

for the annual meeting, and I was not much if any better; but I went in the name of the Lord, encouraged by these words, "Whosoever will may come;" "Ask what ye will, and it shall be done;" and "These signs shall follow them that believe; they shall lay hands upon the sick, and they shall recover." These precious promises I claimed for mine. I resolved in my heart I would have a Bible salvation at any cost: which meant death to self, pride, worldly conformity, yea, death to everything contrary to God's word.

The Lord enabled me to reach the camp-ground in safety. The dear saints made a bed for me beside the pulpit, and I lay there during the services, being too weak to sit up long at a time. I commenced seeking God with all my heart, and found him true to his word. He did pardon all my sins, and gave me a clear witness that I was accepted. Then I presented my body a living sacrifice, and died the death unto sin. This was no formal thing, but a real and awful death. A death so painful that it seemed that I should die literally, and God did sanctify my nature, my entire being. O praise the Lord!

Then I felt I was in a condition to ask God to heal my body, which we did. With several others, I was anointed in the name of Jesus, and the elders' hands were laid on us, with prayer for our healing, and God instantly healed my body. Praise his dear name forever! From that time I have been every whit made whole. Able to read, sew, and do house work. God is my strength and my Redeemer. He keeps me healed, soul and body, and I keep my healing just as I keep my salvation, by a constant trust and faith in God. I have been wonderfully tested at times regarding my healing. About two months after, I had worked quite hard one day and brought on my weak and bad feelings again. Then the enemy suggested that I had lost my healing. For some time I suffered in mind and body, not knowing just how to trust God over all these bad feelings. But God saw my trouble and sent me the needed counsel. Sister Courtney instructed me to still regard myself a well woman, and rest up from the effects of overworking. This was a good lesson to me, and I never forgot it. I was feeling so weak and bad it seemed I was unable to wash dishes. But I went to my room, knelt down before God and said, "Father, I know you have healed me, now I want you to retouch my body with the healing power, and increase my faith." Then I went to work in the name of Jesus, and my bad feelings all left me. Praise the Lord! After that when my eyes and body would feel bad, I pitched in and read and worked the more, and I would look up and say "Father, I know I am healed, and when you see I am not afraid to trust you regardless of symptoms, take the bad feelings away," and they would soon go. So I have learned by experience how to trust God to keep me well, as well as to keep me saved.

I have been healed many times of different afflictions since my first healing. Once the Lord instantly raised me up from a very sick condition with the measles.

I have been working for God for nearly six years, assisting in meetings night and day. Sometimes we travel over land with conveyance sixty miles a day, and God wonderfully strengthens me, so that I can stand it about as well as the strongest persons.

Praise the Lord! I enjoy good health now, God's rich blessings in my soul, and complete victory over all the world, and the powers of evil, and I give God all the glory.

35 Fountain St.,   FRANKIE MILLER.
Batttle Creek, Mich.

MOTHERHOOD.

Believing it duty as well as privilege to acknowledge God's kindness in his dealings with me, and knowing mothers especially need encouragement to cast all their care and burdens upon the Lord, I give my experience in healing.

When I was converted, over nine years ago, a degree of faith for healing was given me, and my general health was much improved. But after a year had passed, very alarming symptoms of stomach trouble appeared. So intense was the distress that I was obliged to sit up all the latter part of the night for a week. Having had no teaching on faith healing, I was soon consulting a physician, who said my case was severe, and I must take a course of treatment. This alarmed me more because my older brother had suffered intensely for several years with the disease, making us think it an inherited trouble from our grandfather. So the medicine was procured and tested for several days, satisfactorily for immediate relief. Placing the bottle on a window above the table, where as I worked my eyes would light upon it, and this conversation took place: "Do you belong to God?" "Yes, soul and body." "But as soon as your body is in trouble, you go to the devil—(wicked doctors) to make you well—is this wisdom?" "If your body belongs to God, why not let him care for it?"

After this I could not bear to take the medicine, and even the sight of it was offensive; so I soon threw it away, that I might not be tempted to take it when in distress. Several days after, while in distress, I walked the room trying to throw myself

OF SOUL AND BODY

fully into God's hands for healing. But it seemed I grew worse, and symptoms of every disease I ever had filled my body so I was one mass of pains and aches. As the day was closing, I stepped before the window, and as I beheld the hills, this thought burst upon my mind and heart—It is easier for these hills to pass away than for God's word to fail. Therefore, it is done, my BODY IS the LORD'S, and he is able to KEEP all we entrust to him. No thoughts of feeling—but in a moment all distress was gone and I felt new, strong and active, and had a consciousness that my body was the Lord's, peculiarly pure, and thereafter dearer to me, as it was worthy of God's touch and care. My faith was afterward tried, but when I could REJOICE in the trial, victory came very speedily.

After I was sanctified my faith was much increased, and every trouble was then taken to the Lord. Then no wonder that shortly before motherhood's most trying hour, that divine help, strength and endurance should be sought for, and that our kind loving Lord should whisper, "I'll do better for you than you can ask or think." Or that the words of King David, in Psalms 22: 9, should be received with new power. Bless our God! who causeth us always to triumph But it was on the third day after deliverance that he made known *how much better* he would do for me than I could think. All that morning these words kept coming to my mind, and after reading the instance of healing in Matt. 9: 20–23, the real force of the words dawned upon my soul and I said, "I am healed; I can in the name of the Lord arise." As I spoke, my body was shaken as if it were a leaf, and the enemy said, "There! you are having a nervous chill." But I said, Get thee hence, Satan; this is the Lord's healing power. So at the first opportunity, with a little waiting upon, I arose, giving praise to God, walking the room with my "little blessing" in my arms; appeared at the supper table, much to the surprise of the head of the family, who has just returned from the field, but was perfectly satisfied when told that the Lord was with us in healing power.

The next morning I arose as usual, as it was wash day, and the work was crowded. Three beds were made, and three rooms swept, then a sponge cake and cup custards made for cold supper, and I was washing the dinner dishes as a neighbor sister came to care for the little one. She was so surprised that all she could say was: "Well, it is all the Lord's doings, and is marvelous in our eyes." And we rejoiced together in his goodness. The blessing upon my soul was wonderful whenever I told my experience of healing. Worldly wisdom shook her head and whispered, "You'll be sorry for this simple freak." But we rejoiced the more in the knowledge that our Lord had lifted us over three weeks of weakness, and had told us to be strong in him, and he never makes a mistake.

Once more have we relied upon Him in this hour of greatest need, and again has he done better for me than I could "ask or think," healing me on the second day, giving me strength to do what in the eyes of the world was madness and folly; but bless the Lord, we do know it is good to trust in God, and know that he is able and willing to do much more for us as our faith increases. Dear sisters, may this little testimony of God's faithfulness and compassion encourage every one to come boldly to the throne of grace to find help in every time of need.

In the love of Jesus,

JENNIE C. RUTTY.

HE HEALETH OUR DISEASES.

DEAR SAINTS AND ALL THE AFFLICTED EVERYWHERE: "Whatsoever ye do, do all to the glory of God."—1 Cor. 10: 31. It is my duty to testify to the wonderful power of God, through faith on our part, to heal our bodies of all diseases, that they may be pure temples for the indwelling of the Holy Spirit.

After the Lord had pardoned my sins I consecrated

all to him. He then tried me upon nearly all that my consecration covered. He asked me, as he did Abraham, to give up my only son, who was then about one year of age; his mother having died after having been treated by six doctors. After she died I sent him to Iowa to my brother. One day I received a message stating that baby had been given up by the doctor to die of catarrhal fever. I prayed that if it was the will of the Lord he would heal him, and received the answer then and there according to I Jno. 5: 15. The next day I received a message which read: " Baby is out of danger." For the prayer of faith shall save the sick, and the Lord shall raise him up.—James 5: 15 Later I sprained my wrist badly, but I sought unto the Lord, and not unto the physicians (2 Chron. 16: 12), and was healed.

The face of our youngest boy had been a mass of sores for many months, caused by tetter. Yet the Lord, through faith in him, has taken it all away. For He said, " I will take sickness away from the midst of thee."—Ex. 23: 25. And he doeth all things well.

Our eldest boy was troubled with worms, and we dosed him with pink-root and senna, all to no avail, never thinking that the Lord would heal such a simple disease. But after he had become very weak we bowed our heads in prayer for his recovery. And the Lord healed him, and he has never been troubled with worms since. "All things are possible to him that believeth."—Mark 9: 23.

He healed my wife of weak back instantaneously, and said, "Thy faith hath made thee whole."—Luke 8:48. He healed my mother of a very troublesome disease, after she had trusted in doctors to no avail. "But they that wait upon the Lord shall renew their strength."—Psa. 40: 31.

May all who read these testimonies bear in mind that the Lord has not forsaken the earth, and that the days of miracles are not past. But remember, dear people, that he who said, "Lo, I am with you alway, even unto the end of the world," is still in the midst of his peculiar people. Praise his name forever!

Your brother, clothed and in his right mind.

JNO. E. ROBERTS.
Denver, Colo., 1945 Downing Ave., *Aug. 10, 1891.*

TOUCHED WITH POWER DIVINE.

DEAR READERS: I believe it will be to the glory of God for me to tell of his wonderful healing power. My soul magnifies his great name for his mercy and goodness, not only for the healing of the body, but for healing my sin-sick soul, which was in darkness and despair. He has delivered my soul from the power of Satan, and brought me into His marvelous light by the application of the precious blood of the Son of God. I am saved and sanctified by a second work of grace; fully saved from inbred depravity by his mighty Spirit of power. Praise God!

When my body was healed I was all given up to God. On the 27th day of August, 1887, I was taken sick with chills and fever; also other diseases set in at an alarming rate. Those who cared for me realized that I needed as much attention at night as in the day-time. My strength had so completely left me that it seemed that I would never be able to speak to any one who came into the room. I would breathe a prayer for the Lord God to help me before I could utter a syllable. And so utterly helpless had I become with regard to using my arms and hands that I entreated God from time to time to help me to move them. I was in a perfectly helpless condition most of the time.

During the first two weeks of my illness a dear sister in Christ administered to my wants in the meekness of Jesus, and urged me to have hands laid on me for my healing. One of the brethren who has the gift of healing was sent for, and they laid on hands and I was greatly relieved. Praise God! A few days later a minister came and laid on hands for my recovery, and yet the Lord did not seem to answer prayer for my immediate recovery. I was at the home of the sister who was caring for me, who lived at Kendall, Mich. And the Lord showed me it was his will for me to return to my home in Battle Creek, which was a number of miles away, and a trip to be taken by railway. But the Lord greatly increased our faith, and by parental aid I returned home.

Shortly after my arrival a physician was called without my knowledge of it until he came into the house. He soon saw that I had no desire to take medicine, and soon went away. I did not improve any, and the third day another one came. The devil made me think that I ought to take medicine, and I took two doses to please my parents. But God visited me in a wonderful manner, and impressed me to take no more; and if I would trust him he would complete the healing. The next time the physician came I told him that I was all on the altar, and I would take the Lord for my physician, and he said that "the soul is on the altar, but the body is not." And God impressed me to look at Rom. 12: 1:—"I beseech you therefore, brethren, by the mercies of God that ye present your bodies a living sacrifice, holy, acceptable unto God, which is your reasonable service." These blessed words are a direct contradiction to his statement. I saw he was unskillful in the scriptures and did not feel led to say much to him. He was indignant when told that I could take no more of his medicine; and said he would come the next morning and inject it under the skin, which would be very painful for me. But God in his wonderful wisdom prevented his calling on me again. I did not improve any, but continued to pray to the Lord to heal me, until one day I heard a voice from heaven say, "Get up." I realized my critical condition, how utterly helpless I was, and could not rise. Although I believed the Lord saved me to the uttermost; and yet did not give up praying for him to give me the healing faith and to heal me.

All during my illness it was my earnest desire to know that God did the work of healing all himself, which I was confident he was able to do, for all things are possible with God.

While praying with intense earnestness some time afterward, I heard the same voice from heaven speak to me, "Get up." And yet I continued to look at awful condition, which was perfect helplessness. A day later one afternoon towards evening when my suffering was greater than I had ever experienced in my life, I gave up all hope of living any longer, and told my mother that I was ready to go home. Praise God! I was ready.

But within an hour from this time I heard the same still small voice from heaven speak to me for the third and last time, " Get up."

I immediately arose from my bed and walked. I was touched with power divine—the real healing power of God. Praise his great name forever! The work was done in a moment.

Then came the trial of my faith. Praise God for the trials! I well remember one day while walking that I became so very weak that it seemed almost impossible for me to take another step. But I heard a voice from heaven say, " Claim it." And I immediately claimed the healing power of God, and my strength was increased. Praise his name!

At another time symptoms of chills came upon me at such a rate that my teeth began to chatter, and I was unable to control myself. But the Lord assured me that it was his will for me to claim the healing power, which I did, and God gave me the victory in my soul. And so he led me from victory to victory until the enemy was completely defeated. His blessed word assures us that the trial of our faith is more precious than gold. Blessed be his name!

Yours in him.

MAY SMITH.

Battle Creek, Mich., No. 27 North Ave., *Sept. 15,1891.*

DIVINE HEALING

A TRIAL OF FAITH.

For the glory of God, and to encourage the afflicted I write the following: My health failed me very mysteriously, and I suffered from a continued decline year after year, until my disease—which was internal—became chronic, and after five years my eyes failed me in sympathy with a general nerve weakness, and though not blind or entirely helpless, yet I was not able to read a page, or sew a yard of cloth for nearly ten years. I was shut out from the world, as it were, until the time promised when God should pour out his Spirit upon all flesh, and set the captives free.

Seven years ago I heard of a people called the saints, " who went up to the feast" yearly at Bangor, to worship God in the good old way; and that God was saying to the remnant of the camp of Israel in these latter days: " Go forward," for from henceforth " I will be in the midst of thee." I heard of mighty works being wrought through the name of the holy child Jesus, and I said in my soul, " If God permits I will touch the hem of his garment and be made whole." Another meeting three months later found me at the same place where I presented myself for the healing of my eyes. God had a second work in view, and because of this, and for my good, he permitted me to come especially with desire for the healing of my eyes at this time. I had suffered more with my eyes than otherwise for a long time, and had been obliged to rest my body, until I fancied that with their recovery I would feel quite well. God heard and answered prayer, and with the laying on of hands in the name of the Lord, in the instant of the exercise of faith, I reached for a fine print Bible which was lying near me, and read nearly two chapters without harm.

Praises be unto God forever and ever! I returned to my Northern home, and began to undertake the demands of the same, when within one week I began to realize the original disease was being aggravated with my effort to labor, and that I needed an entire healing. I was two hundred miles from any one I knew who had a living faith. And as my condition became worse and worse I cried mightily to God to deliver me from all infirmity. I tried to pray believingly, but when an ache or a pain followed I thought, Surely God has not healed me or I would not feel so. Several weeks passed, when at a time of much suffering, I was led to set apart a time for fasting, the same as they did at Bangor. I asked God to reveal to me what was lacking on my part, and while waiting thus before him I was led to take up a GOSPEL TRUMPET which I had not read. My eyes first rested upon the experience of a sister who had been healed of the same disease. She said that when hands were laid upon her for healing she was in great pain, and afterwards she was still in pain, but according to God's word she was healed. He gave her strength to get up and go about, and as she continued to believe, strength was given, and the pain passed away. She said at one time she was again in pain, and she asked the Lord why it was. He showed her that it was not the old disease, but only a test of her faith. Also at another time when a sense of weariness came on without cause, that it was not the old disease, but only a test of her faith, all of which passed away when her faith was lifted above her feelings. And that we must not ask God to heal us and then "wait to see," but "get up," and do as if we had what we have asked for.

All this was like a message from heaven to me. My prayer was answered. I read the same twice over, and then fell upon my knees with my paper in my hand, and asked God to touch me with his healing power, and make me every whit whole. I claimed what I had asked for, and arose declaring within myself that I was healed, with no other evidence than God's word. That was enough, and I was indeed made whole from that hour. I expected to be tested in some way, as this sister had been, but having gained a knowledge concerning physical temptations, I felt that I was fully armed for the conflict, and with the armor of faith I should win the battle.

The dear Lord permitted me to soar along in my happy freedom for six weeks without an ache or a pain; when suddenly, while preparing a testimony of my healing for publication, I felt a sharp pain in my brain, which had formerly been in a state of congestion much of the time in the years past. Oh how natural it felt! and soon another throb came on the other side. Just then the Spirit reminded me of the lesson I had learned on physical temptations, and I looked up and said within myself, Father, I'm healed. Test me and try me all I have need, but give me strength to continue my labor, and when I am tested enough, deliver me from every symptom of disease.

I was not doing more than was reasonable for a well person to do, so I guaged my ability on the line of perfect health. Had I laid aside my writing, or flinched in the least in that hour, I should have been overcome again. But praise God! I gloried in the discipline which he led me through, and gained a wonderful victory in both soul and body.

Several months after this I was writing a letter, when suddenly I felt a pain in one of my eyes. In an instant I was reminded again that another trial was at hand. The pain came again and again; and as before, I looked up and said, "Father, I'm healed; test me and try me all I have need, only give me strength in these eyes to continue my writing and whatever is needful for me to do." I kept on writing for a half hour or so, when I had to lay it by to get supper, after which I was about to resume the same, when the enemy suggested like this: "It has grown dark since you left your writing, and it would be presumption for one to try to write by "lamp light," with pains passing through their eyes, as yours are." I said to myself, I am perfectly well. Yes, "every whit made whole," and it is for me to do as well people do; help me, Lord, to triumph in this trial. I continued my writing as long as I desired, giving no heed to the pains which came now and then, only in prayerful uplifting for strength to endure all that should be permitted to come upon me. During the night I felt the pain two or three times.

On rising in the morning a tear flowed from one eye as though it were quite weak, but I committed them to God, and went about my work as though nothing was the matter, and the pain and weakness all passed away, so that I really forgot it while absorbed in my work, until afternoon, when I was reminded of my former condition. Praise God! it was a glorious victory, and a blessing to my soul and body also. I have been afflicted in various ways at certain times during the years which have passed by, but God has been my physician and my constant deliverer from all the powers of the enemy. And I will ever praise his precious name for what he has done for me.

A sister in Christ.

Mrs. J. E. Courtney.

Bay View, Mich.

MARVELOUS HEALING OF THE SOUL.

Feeling it a great privilege as well as a duty I owe to God, and believing it another opportunity the Lord has given me to glorify him, to testify to his wonderful power to save and heal, resting assured it is his will, as I was so deeply impressed by the Spirit to add my testimony with the many others that will fill these pages, permit me to say, although others of his children may have had as rich an experience, none have ever received a richer than I, or been more wonderfully blessed, both soul and body.

I was an invalid for fifteen long years; and suffered during that time with untold sufferings. Being ignorant of God's power to heal the body, I, of course, was brought under the care of earthly physicians, who did all in their power to relieve me, but all to no avail.

I spent over three thousand dollars trying to find relief, and at last was much worse than when I began. Everything was done that a loving mother's heart and hand could plan. I was sent to the Cleveland Water Cure, also to the Surgical Institute at Indianapolis, and there braced from head to foot in steel, hoping to take away the pressure of my spine, which had become so inflamed I could not raise my head, besides placing myself under the care of all physicians within reach of home.

At last through the providence of God I was led to go to Michigan as a last resort, hoping the climate might prove beneficial, but the Lord had another way of bringing back life to this almost dead body. Instead of gaining, I grew worse and worse, and when I had been in Petoskey one year and two months, the dear Lord had compassion upon me, and in my extreme helplessness manifested his power and raised me from the bed upon which I was dying. My friends were watching to see the last breath, and all earthly hope was gone.

If any one has ever doubted the power and willingness of God to heal the body, I can assure them if they had ever passed through my experience, they could never doubt it again. I take the liberty to say: Divine healing is a reality, and the Lord is willing to heal those who believe.

I was healed on the 28th day of July, 1883, at Petoskey, Mich., over six hundred miles from my home. It would take a book to tell all the wonderful things the Lord has done for me, and the blessed way in which he has led me. It seems I must have been a very stubborn child, for I had to be torn all to pieces, as it were, before I could take the Lord as my healer.

Seven physicians had given me up as a hopeless case, and the dear Lord showed me there was no hope except in him. Many, many times he would speak these words to me over my bed: "Trust in the Lord, all else will fail;" and "If thou wouldst believe, thou shouldst see the glory of God." He also gave me many promises from his word, through his Holy Spirit, to encourage and strengthen my faith.

When the divine touch came, I arose from my bed, dressed myself, and as I began to walk—which I had not done for all those years—how forcibly these words came to me, and seemed to be stamped in large gold letters on my heart: "Fear thou not, for I am with thee; be not dismayed, for I am thy God. I will help thee, I will strengthen thee; yea I will uphold thee with the right hand of my righteousness." And the fourth day after I was healed, as I was going to take a short journey, and feeling my need of divine help, these words were again given me: "Have not I commanded thee? be strong, and of good courage; be not afraid, neither be thou dismayed, for the Lord thy God is with thee whithersoever thou goest." O how good the Lord has been to me!

You ask what was the disease? It was very complicated internal disease, with spinal irritation, with extreme nervous prostration, so that for years I could bear no company, not even my own folks, only those who had to administer to my daily wants; and could not bear the sound of a voice or any noise, without causing me to become wild, and could not control myself. My stomach could not take the most simple article of diet without intense pain. I was so low that I could eat only with a teaspoon, and had not eaten a meal at my mother's table for eleven years, until the Lord healed me.

It is now eight years since the Lord healed my body, and I have not taken any medicine in all that time, and to day He gives me strength to fulfill my household duties and care for my aged mother, who so faithfully cared and labored for me through those long, weary years.

I bless God to day for all my affliction, assured that it has given me a home in heaven. I can say with the Psalmist David: "I know, O Lord, that thy judgments are right, and that thou in faithfulness hast afflicted me." And also, "It was good for me that I have been afflicted;" I know now that my will is His will. O how sweet are all our Father's ways when we are swallowed up in the boundless love of Christ! It would be needless to tell you that I am happy.

Although the Lord has done such great things for my body, it is as nothing compared to the work he has done for my soul. As the prophet Malachi puts it: " The Lord opened the windows of heaven to my soul, and poured down a blessing that I was not able to contain." Praise God! that fountain is still flowing. He has given me the joys of salvation, and made me to rejoice with joy unspeakable and full of glory. One year and a half after the Lord healed my body, I was again led back to Michigan through divine guidance. Although converted at the age of sixteen, yet I felt a lack in my soul, and a great desire to be wholly the Lord's. I consecrated my all to God, and received the blessing of holiness. O the heights and depths of God's love I enjoyed! For eight long months I seemed to be lifted out of this world, and soaring in the atmosphere of heaven. My soul exulted in the thought of heaven, and the boundless love of Christ. Truly I had a foretaste of heavenly bliss. I could realize the language of Christ—John 17: 16: "They are not of the world even as I am not of the world." The Lord has truly led me in ways I knew not. He has given me such beautiful visions. I will tell of one, for the glory of God.

While singing a song, "Pearly Gates," I became anxious to know if the gate of heaven was open for me. That evening while in prayer, and my earthly eyes closed, the dear Lord opened my spiritual eyes and showed me a beautiful green path, so very narrow, with hills on either side, disclosing all earthly things from view, commencing on the earth with a gradual ascent, until in the distance it seemed to reach heaven. And at the end of that path I could see a large gate thrown wide open, and the Savior standing with open arms to receive me. Praise God! I could say then I knew the gate of heaven was open for me. It was a glorious scene.

The Lord continues to bless me and fill me with his love, and feed my soul with food from his own table, and enables me to comprehend more and more the wonderful provisions of his grace, and condescension of his children. I am lost in wonder, love and praise when I contemplate the marvelous provision the Lord has made for his own in both temporal and spiritual things, and in preparing us a mansion in the realms of glory. He has even taken the very principles of heaven and formed out of it an immortal soul, and placed it within these temples of his, to live in here upon earth, and glorify his own name. How much it means to be a follower of the meek and lowly Jesus! I have by the grace of God, given up all to follow him. The world has no longer any charms for me since Jesus has been revealed to my heart. Although I am unknown to the world, yet I am well known to him.

Again can I utter the words of David: "I am a wonder unto many, but God is my strong refuge." I find solid comfort in reading God's word. How its pages have been illumined by his Holy Spirit! How precious all the promises, and what peace and rest they bring to those who take them for their own! It seems to me there is comfort enough in two or three to satisfy every longing soul, and lull it to rest. For instance: "Come unto me, all ye that labor and are heavy laden, and I will give you rest." "Cast all your care upon him, for he careth for thee." "I will never leave thee, nor forsake thee;" and, "Thou wilt keep him in perfect peace, whose mind is stayed on thee"

How rich and full these words are to every child of God. I do thank the Lord that he has made me free to enjoy him here, with the sweet assurance in my heart, of life eternal with him on high. It is delightful to know we are destined to live forever, and that natural death is the gate to endless life, and life is secured to us by virtue of our relation to him who is eternal. "Because I live ye shall live also." May the Lord bless these words to the good of all who read and use them for his glory.

Yours redeemed by the blood, and happy in a Savior's love.

MARY R. MALCOMSON.

Vevay, Ind., *July 25, 1891.*

THE FAMILY PHYSICIAN.

In the month of August, 1884, we received the light of holiness, through the GOSPEL TRUMPET, and a holiness teacher who came into our neighborhood. And we heard of a people that the signs follow, as we read of in James 5, and Mark 16. Our first experience in the healing power was a few months after we were wholly sanctified. Our little boy who was about a year and a half of age, one night was suddenly taken with the croup, and awakened us with his struggles to get his breath. But instead of using medicines, or an earthly physician, we did not so much as light a lamp, or get out of bed, but took his case to the Lord in silent prayer, and before we got through praying for him, his struggles for breath all stopped, and the child was well and went to sleep.

Oh how near the dear Lord did seem to us that night! It was wonderful! How it increased our faith in the mighty power of God! At that time we had about twenty-five different kinds of medicine in the house, but after that my wife emptied all her medicines on the ground, and the Lord has been our physician ever since.

In the year 1885 we had the blessed privilege of attending the Bangor camp-meeting, and my wife was healed of diseases which she had had for twenty-two years, and which had baffled the skill of all the best doctors we could hear of and consult. Praise the Lord! It would take too much space to tell of all the cases of healing in our family which the Lord has performed. He is our constant family physician, and a very present help in time of trouble.

Your wholly saved brother, made white and tried.

WILLIAM STOWELL.

Coopersville, Mich, *Sept. 10, 1891.*

HEALED OF RHEUMATISM AND A STIFF JOINT.

There are a great many persons who do not believe in faith healing in these days, as taught in the Word of God, and in fact I never believed much in it until I saw the power of God manifested in healing the sick and then found it was according to his word. Now I know of a truth that God does manifest his power in these days in healing the sick, for I have not only seen others made well through faith in him, but have myself received the divine touch which swept all disease from my body. A little over a year ago I was attacked with La Grippe, and after being sick four days, pneumonia set in, followed by inflammatory rheumatism.

For about two months my fingers, arms, lower limbs and neck were drawn up in such a manner that I could not during that time get off the bed only as lifted. At times I could straighten myself for awhile. This turned to muscular rheumatism, with shooting pains from joint to joint. From my first sickness my left hip became stiff, and the cords of my left leg became so contracted that one leg was shorter than the other. My kidneys became affected during my sickness, also my lungs were so bad that the doctor said I had the consumption. Four or five doctors waited upon me from time to time. Soon all medicine failed. O the pain and suffering I passed through and had to endure, cannot be told!

But the suffering of my body was not all. I had a sin-sick soul, and knew that if I died it would be in my sins; yet I knew God was able to save all who would come unto him. I knew no medicine would cure me. I knew of a lady in South Haven whom the Lord had instantaneously healed while she was lying at the point of death with consumption. I felt that if the Lord would heal one person, he surely would heal others. But I was not in a condition to be healed, as my soul was not saved. Knowing of the sickness of this woman, and how near the door of death she was, and how wonderful was her deliverance, I began to take courage, and felt like trusting God, and the Lord soon permitted me to improve some in health, yet I was a great sufferer.

In February, 1891, I was visiting some friends for a few days, after which I started for my home in Pine Grove. As I passed the TRUMPET office in Grand Junction, something seemed to tell me to go in; and in my weakness I started staggering along, and as I entered I met the busy workers of the Lord, and soon made known my errand. They told me the first thing was to get salvation and then the Lord would heal me. All work was stopped, and as they gathered in a small room, in a very few minutes the Lord pardoned my sins. I was then instructed regarding going on unto perfection, as taught in the Word of God; and if I could not exercise proper faith to be healed, come back when the Lord led. From that moment I began to amend.

In about three weeks I returned to the office, and there in an upper room, in the presence of two or three brethren the Lord sanctified my soul, and then I obeyed James 5: 14, 15, and was anointed, and the Lord healed my body and I returned home and went to work knowing the Lord had done the work of healing.

Several weeks after, some pains began to come upon me—as I was a night watchman, and exposed to the night air so much—and thus the enemy of my soul tried to get me to doubt my healing. I again called upon the brethren and was anointed, and the Lord witnessed the healing. After returning home the Lord brought to my mind that I had three or four bottles of medicine which I was not using, but had put away in case of an emergency. And I do not doubt but that was why the symptoms came back. The Lord wanted me to throw it away and take him alone, as his grace is an all-sufficiency in every emergency. Glory to God! it was destroyed, and ever since I have had good health and have been able to do a good day's work. My left limb is now as long as the other one, and my hip is well. I spent about all I had, and went in debt nearly one hundred dollars for doctor bills. The Lord gave his treatment without money and without price, yet he required me to consecrate to do his will in all things.

JACOB GRUBER.

Pine Grove, Mich., *June 17, 1891.*

A CRUSHED ARM HEALED.

It is a blessed privilege for me to testify to the mighty saving power of God. Oh! I am praising him for the sweetness and completeness I find in his love. Over four years ago the Lord convicted me of my lost and undone condition, and showed me that I must spend eternity with God, or spend it with all the wicked in the regions of the lost world. Before I came to God I could not rest, day nor night. I felt miserable on account of my sins, and fell upon my knees and cried, "God be merciful to me a sinner," and promised him that I would serve him all the days of my life. And when I repented of my sins he forgave them all. For the first time in my life I could say I was the Lord's child. The next night I came to the Lord and " presented my body a living sacrifice, holy, acceptable unto God," which was my reasonable service, and the Lord sanctified me wholly. Oh! the joy I felt no tongue can tell. I was wholly the Lord's and he was mine.

I was the only one of our family that was saved, so I was tried and persecuted at home, but Jesus was my helper, and in him I put my trust, and realized his grace was sufficient at all times.

DIVINE HEALING

I also felt the call to go and work for Jesus. We read in the Word of God that he has chosen the weak things of this world to confound the mighty. I knew the hand of God was upon me to go forth and warn sinners to flee the wrath to come, and he gave me a willingness to leave friends and home and work in the vineyard of the Lord. For the last two years I have been out upon the battle-field of the Lord, rescuing perishing souls, and he has supplied all my needs, both spiritually and temporally. And I can also testify to his mighty healing power. I used to be afflicted very much, but when the Lord saved me he showed me that all things are possible with God. He is able to heal both soul and body. Since being out in the work of the Lord I have met with some accidents, one of which I will mention.

Last winter, a year ago, at Windsor, Mo., while riding in a wagon, it was upset off the end of a bridge, and we all fell several feet with the wagon upon us. My head was hurt very bad, and my right arm crushed, and I was helpless. They carried me into the house, and my sufferings were so great that I thought I would die. I had two hard chills. The dear saints called upon the Lord, and laid hands on my head, and the Lord healed my head, and gave me faith for the healing of my crushed arm. That very night the Lord touched my body with his mighty healing power, and I was healed. I used to think God could heal all but broken bones, but now I know he can even do that; for his power on that line has been tested in my case. I have testified to hundreds of people, of this mighty healing power, although some will not believe. God knows I testify only for his glory. Some would even come to me and tell me that if I would say my arm was only hurt, and not crushed, more would believe it. Well, I cannot limit the power of God. It is wonderful to know what God will do for his children who keep themselves humble before him.

Your sister kept by power divine.

LODEMA KASER.

HEALED OF TUMOR.

BRO. BYRUM: As I have learned that you are intending to publish a work on divine healing, I desire to glorify God by telling of his wonderful power to heal the body in these last days. I can say to the glory of God that he has healed me of an ovarian tumor of seven or eight years growth. He healed me about four years ago, and since that time I have not been troubled with it. Giving God all the glory, I remain his child.

MARY SMITH.

Dushville, *Sept. 7, 1891*

AT DEATH'S DOOR.

To the glory of God I wish to tell what the dear Lord has done for us. In 1888, my mother, Mrs. S. Cunningham, was taken very sick with pneumonia fever, and became so weak and low that she could not raise nor turn her head. She bade us all good bye, and we thought she was dying. Bro. Gray anointed her with oil and laid on hands, and while we prayed she sat up in bed and clapped her hands, and the next evening got up and walked to the other bed, and next morning went to the table and ate her breakfast. She was so low that she did not know when we began to pray for her. Although she was seventy years of age, yet the Lord restored her to health.

I was troubled for nine years with an inward tumor, and was healed by faith in God, and the laying on of hands, by Bro. Warner and Mother Smith, for which I give God all the glory.

Our daughter nine years of age was taken very sick with neuralgia of the stomach, inflammation of the bowels, and rheumatism all over her body. We had one of the best physicians wait on her for four weeks, and to prevent her having spasms, kept her under the influence of morphine. Her sufferings were intense. At the end of four weeks I felt led of God to lay aside all medicines and take God for her healing. I wrote to Bro. D. S. Warner to pray for her. After giving a dose of medicine one morning, I felt impressed to give her no more, so we quit giving it and had the doctor no more. I said, "Lord, here is my child, I leave her in thy hands, live or die. Just thy will be done and I will say, Amen."

About three o'clock in the afternoon she said to me, "Mamma, I am healed. Give me something to eat." She had eaten scarcely anything for four weeks. I asked her how she knew she was healed, and she replied, "I have the witness."

The Lord did not reveal to me that he was going to heal her, but I was waiting and trusting, perfectly resigned to his will, whatever it might be. She sat up next morning. and her strength came gradually, but her pain ceased instantly. Such a physician is worthy of all honor and praise. Glory to his name!

Your sister in Jesus.

SALLIE ROGERS.

Humboldt, Kan., *Sept. 20, 1891.*

HEART DISEASE CURED.

DEAR BRO. E. E. BYRUM: About eight years ago I had lung disease so bad that it seemed I could not live much longer. My husband wrote to one of the best doctors in New York City, and gave a detailed description of my case. He answered that he could not cure me, but might possibly help me. This alarmed my husband and he did not show me the letter until we were both fully saved, then he read it to me. I told him I was ready to die. But shortly after this, by the laying on of hands, and by faith and prayer to God, I was instantly healed. All pain was gone, and my coughing stopped, and I became stout and healthy again.

In about a year from that time, while overburdened with work, I was severely attacked with heart disease. My sufferings were intense, and my case was soon pronounced incurable. I went to the Great Physician, "who healeth all our diseases," and he healed me, and poured out his blessings upon my soul, and made me free from all pain and disease. To him be all the praise.

Your sister saved in Jesus.

MRS. L. MARKWELL.

Wichita, Kan., *July 3, 1891.*

HEALED OF CATARRH.

BRO. BYRUM: I feel led to write my experience to be published for the glory of God.

Three years ago the 22nd of May, the dear Lord wonderfully healed my afflicted body. I went to the Ridgeville, O., grove-meeting; was first converted, then sanctified, and two days later instantly healed by the mighty power of God, by anointing and the laying on of hands. To God be all the glory. The healing power was felt all through me, and I knew the instant it was done, and can never thank Him enough for his goodness to me. I was afflicted for years with lung difficulty, catarrh and other ailments.

Two bottles of medicine were taken with me to the meeting, but were of no use, for there I found a wonderful Physician who healed me of all my diseases. Praise his name! I had a very bad cough, and after I was healed it was not all gone, but I knew the Lord had healed me and it was all right. But my Methodist sister doubted my healing because I coughed some yet. I took it to the Lord in prayer, and asked him to remove the cough, that they might believe. Thanks be to God! the third time I prayed it was all gone. I was weak but he gave me strength that enabled me to do my work and washing. If I felt weak I would ask God for strength. If Satan tempted, I would command him to depart. From that day to this I have not taken the least bit of any kind of medicine. He has healed me, soul and body. Oh, what an unspeakable joy we find in trusting God for all things! He is a present help in every time of need. My prayer is that every afflicted one will just believe with all their heart, and it shall be done. First get saved, and then God will give the faith.

      Mrs. Christina Lederer.
Watervliet, Mich., *Aug. 31, 1891.*

HEALED OF CANCER.

Dear Bro. Byrum: In the year 1883 I discovered that I was afflicted with cancer. At that time I was converted, but knew nothing about holiness, or this blessed evening light, but was in perfect submission to the will of God, to live or die. On Jan. 11, 1884, I submitted to a very severe surgical operation. It brought me very near death's door, yet for four weeks I got along very nicely, after which I passed through a severe ordeal and was given up to die, but after three months the Lord saw fit to raise me up from my bed of affliction.

In 1887 my health began to fail again, and after consulting the family physician he said the cancer had come back again, and he thought there could be nothing more done for me. However, he went with me to Pittsburg, to see what could be done. He took me to a leading physician of that city, who pronounced my case a hopeless one, and delivered a lecture over me to one hundred or more students, declaring my hopeless condition; and intimated that I would not live one year.

OF SOUL AND BODY.

I always believed that Jesus had power to heal, and that he was just as willing to do it now, as in the days of the apostles. And when the doctors said there could be nothing more done for me, something seemed to say to me: Man can do no more, but God can. And I believed in my heart that God would heal me. I did not begin to pray for healing, but kept believing that he would heal me, and did not seem to get much worse.

One year later I heard holiness preached, and the Lord sanctified my soul. Then I began to pray after this manner: Lord, if thou hast laid thine afflicting hand upon me, please remove it. But I received no answer. One day it came to me that the Lord had not afflicted me, but that it was the works of the devil, and I cried: Lord, destroy the works of the devil. Immediately I had the witness that it was done. However, the pain did not cease, neither did the lump disappear. Although I suffered much I did not doubt my healing, and thought God must be trying my faith. I took a great amount of morphine to relieve the pain, and when I was sanctified the people said I was a good woman, but morphine had deluded me. When I heard this I said, If taking morphine brings reproach on the cause of Christ, I will take no more if I die. I was soon severely attacked with intense pain and sickness. The doctor came and tried to compel me to take the morphine, but I would not take it, but was willing for God to handle my case, which he did very successfully. The lump suddenly disappeared, and I have not had a bad attack since; and I have been free from cancer since that time, and am now enjoying the best of health. Blessed be the name of the Lord.

Your sister, sanctified to do the whole will of God

SARAH A. FARRIS.

Butler, Pa., *Sept. 14, 1891.*

RESTORATION OF EYESIGHT.

For seven years I was a great sufferer on account of the affliction of my eyes. There would be weeks at a time that I would be obliged to sit in a dark room, just letting in a very little light, and then my eyes would pain me so that for many days I was obliged to sit by my bed with my head buried in a pillow, in order to get any relief at all. For about two years there had been a film forming over my left eye, nearly covering the pupil. I could not see to read the headings of the newspapers with it, and I could not see to read a chapter in the Bible with my right eye; it was so badly inflamed. I was converted several years before this, and when I prayed I would ask God to give me faith to believe that he would heal them, but he withheld it because I was not where he could do anything for me. I was trying to serve God, yet I was serving the world. But when he let the light of full salvation shine into my soul, and I walked in the light, he gave me faith to believe that he could and would heal them.

After I was sanctified, one Sunday, at the close of the services, I told the brethren that I had faith to be healed. The elder replied: "So have I;" and as we knelt in prayer, he laid his hands upon me and asked the Lord to heal my eyes. When we arose from our knees the film was all gone, and the inflammation was gone from my right eye. God has kept them healed from that day to this.

I can see to read by sun light or lamp light for hours at a time, without the least inconvenience. The Lord still keeps me saved. Praise his name forever!

Your sister in Christ.

ADDIE COON.

Toquin, Mich., *Aug. 2, 1891.*

NASAL CATARRH INSTANTLY HEALED.

DEARLY BELOVED SAINTS: In the year 1887 I gave my heart to God, and after serving the Lord for over four years, I was brought to a test of my faith on account of my afflictions. Having been a sufferer from nasal catarrh for over twenty-two years, during which time I was deprived of the sense of smelling, and as I was on my way to the camp-meeting at Bangor, Mich., I contracted a severe cold, which greatly increased my afflictions and caused much pain, and the mucus was passing down upon my lungs, making me unfit for the ministerial work in which I was engaged, and I saw that I was in danger of that death visitor, consumption.

On the morning of the 15th of June, 1891, while at the meeting, I went out into the woods and bowed before my heavenly Father, and poured out my heart in prayer to him, when the gentle voice said: "Call for the elders and have them anoint you with oil, and lay on hands, and you shall be healed." Leaving the spot, I came to the camp, called for the elders, and within five minutes was healed. In about half an hour afterward I thought I would test my healing. Going into the boarding tent, I picked up a beautiful rose, and as I put it to my nose my heart bounded, as I smelled the sweet odor of that beautiful rose, after having been deprived of such a privilege for over twenty-two years. But God shall have all the glory.

Yours in him.

JOHN A. DILLON.

St. Petersburg, Pa., *Aug. 10, 1891.*

OF SOUL AND BODY.

A WONDERFUL CURE OF CONSUMPTION.

The dear Lord has brought me up from such depths of weakness and affliction, suffering and discouragements, into his great and glorious light, and saves and so lovingly keeps me day by day, that I feel that I should tell it for his glory, and with the hope and desire that it may encourage and lead some other sick and despairing soul to the great and mighty Physician, who so tenderly soothes and heals both soul and body.

I have nursed and buried my whole family, consisting of husband and five children. Also two grandchildren, who were all victims of that terrible disease, consumption. The last of the family, my beloved son, was taken from me about eight month ago, during whose sickness and death I was brought low with nervous prostration and extreme grief. I used medicines until I found they were of no earthly use to me, and I kept growing weaker and weaker.

A slow and lingering fever, a severe cough, and a horrible feeling of suffocation caused by inflammation of the bronchial tubes, caused me to give up all hopes of life. All those symptoms kept increasing. I coughed harder, had pain in my side and chest continually; sometimes sharp and cutting, sometimes dull and aching; chills in the fore part of the day, and in the afternoon hectic fever; terrible night sweats, profuse expectoration, loss of appetite, swelling of the limbs, etc., which, beyond all doubts, were the last stages of consumption.

This was my condition, when on the 14th of March, 1891, Bro. J. W. Byers of this city, called to see me, and asked me if I was a child of God; to which I could truthfully answer, Yes. When he told me that God had provided for the healing of the body as well as for the soul, and that God is not the author of disease, and would heal all who would comply with his requirements, and grasp the promise of healing, I said, Yes, I believe those promises for healing as much as any of the rest of God's word, but did not seem to claim them for myself. This dear brother dealt very plainly with me in taking me through a searching consecration. And when I saw the requirements in order to believe, I was sure I could lay hold on the blessed Master, and never let go until I was sanctified and healed.

I was willing and ready to be anointed for healing Accordingly four of the Lord's elect met in my room at 4 P. M. the next day. The night before this had been a sleepless and restless one on account of my low physical condition, but my faith was strong. These dear saints now offered up earnest prayer, which went up to the throne as incense, and was heard and answered by the Father. I shall never

OF SOUL AND BODY.

forget the sweet consciousness of God's presence filling that little room with a glory not of earth, as my head was anointed with oil. Then once more the promises were claimed for me, his sick and suffering child, while I lay passive at his feet. They began softly to sing: "She only touched the hem of his garment," and O praise his dear name forever! even as they uttered these words the mighty deed was done. Through all my chilled and dying body the warm life-blood went rushing. I felt the glow of a new life; a delicious warmth penetrated my clammy limbs; the pain and soreness left my throat and lungs; I breathed with ease, and raising myself up in bed I stretched out my hands and exclaimed, O thank God, I am healed!

Words cannot be found to express the peace and joy that fills my soul as I realize I am again a well woman. That night my rest was so sweet, and un broken by either cough or sweating; and next morning I arose and dressed myself without assistance; walked through one large room to the front door, looking out upon the beautiful world which I thought I should never see again, then walked back to the kitchen, went to the table and ate a hearty breakfast; for with this new life came a hearty appetite for food. I can now, and have from that day been able to go about my work, often walking half a mile or more to church without fatigue. Blessed and kept "exceeding abundantly above all I could ask or think."

My body is not only healed, but my spiritual life is so wonderfully renewed and strengthened. The dear Lord does graciously fulfill his promise to "keep in perfect peace all those whose minds are stayed on him."

Your sister, sanctified and healed.

ELIZA C. STUBBS.

San Diego, Cal., *June 1, 1891*.

A LITTLE BOY'S PRAYER ANSWERED.

Several years ago I was very much afflicted in body, and was greatly troubled with phthisic, and like hundreds of other people, began doctoring, and had about a bushel-basketful of medicine bottles which I had used. A doctor in Fort Wayne pronounced me incurable, and said I would be a dead man in less than three years, and was liable to drop dead at any time. So I began smoking and chewing tobacco more than ever. I would smoke so I could get breath. I went on in this way for about a year, preaching for the Winebrennarians, and soon two holiness preachers came into the neighborhood, teaching holiness. At first I was foolish enough to oppose them, but soon found they were teaching

Bible doctrine, and I made the consecration, died the death unto sin, and the Lord sanctified my soul on the first day of September, 1876; and at the same time took away the appetite for tobacco, and instantly healed me of phthisic.

About four years after this I was lying sick with typhoid fever, but would take no medicine. A doctor came to see me, and I heard him tell my wife that it was too bad for that man to lie there and die in that way. He went away, and about 10 o'clock I called for a drink of water, and shortly after taking it I felt the effects of something in my stomach, and asked my wife if the doctor left any medicine, but she gave me no answer; I asked the second time, and she said he did. I told her the doctor should have no praise for this; so I put my finger in my throat and threw the stuff off my stomach. Then the Lord impressed me the next morning to send for two of the brethren to come and anoint me with oil, and pray for my healing. They were not elders, and faith healing was not taught there very much, so their faith was not very strong in that direction. But soon they became strong in faith. They anointed me and prayed for me, and I was healed in an instant, and gave God all the praise and glory.

For about five years I had a cancer on my neck below my left ear. In February, 1886, it began eating and causing such awful pain, that my sufferings were intense. My friends advised me to do a great many things; some would advise one thing, some another. This continued until March 6, 1886. In the evening, while alone with my little nine-year-old boy, who had been converted some time before this, I saw that man's extremity was God's opportunity. There in the midst of the most intense suffering, while asking the Lord what I should do, I called little Freddie to me and told him to lay his little hands on the cancer and ask the Lord to take away the pain and heal me. He did so, and prayed to himself. But I said, "Pray aloud so I can hear you." The dear child cried aloud and wept, and said, "Dear Lord, take away the pain and heal Papa;" and in that instant the pain was all gone; and in about four days the cancer was all healed over. The people would say, What did you do to it? I would say, The Lord healed it. They would say, Well, it is healed, sure, but what did you put on it? The Lord healed it, I would say. I was asked as many questions as was the blind man who was restored to sight. "God moves in mysterious ways his wonders to perform."

Dear brethren, see that your boys get saved, and have faith in Jesus Christ, and you will not have to send them through snow and storm and dark nights for a doctor. "O for a faith that will not shrink though pressed by every foe!"

In the year 1890 I had a very severe attack of La Grippe, with a bad cough and awful pain in my side. My friends would get out of patience because I would not have a doctor. Some said it was because I did not want to pay a doctor bill, but I told my son-in-law to take ten dollars of my money, and instead of paying a doctor, after I was dead, to pay it to four poor orphan children. Friends came in to see me die; and made arrangements for my funeral, During the thirteen days of my sickness, my little boy, Freddie, had laid his hands on me six times, and asked the Lord to heal me. In the evening of the fourteenth day of my sickness, while we were alone together, the dear little motherless boy sat weeping, for it seemed as if I was his last friend on earth. I called him to me and he came and kissed me as though it were his farewell kiss. The thought of parting came. O my God! can it be so? After he became a little more quiet I said, Freddie, lay hands on me the seventh time. And he came weeping, and asked the Lord to heal me; and in an instant the pain was all gone, and I was healed. May the Lord receive all the praise.

Your brother in Christ.

J. S. SMURR.

Carlisle, Mich.

HOW GOD DELIVERED ME.

How true are the words of our blessed Master, "A city that is set on a hill cannot be hid." Yea, the overflowing joy of a soul redeemed and purified by the precious blood of Christ will ripple forth from tongue and pen, until the glad tidings are borne all over the land to God's "little ones;" and they are made to rejoice with the angels in heaven, "over one sinner that repenteth."

Ten months have passed away since my captive soul was set at liberty, and the fetters of sin destroyed. But before relating my blessed evening light experience, the dear Lord impresses me to retrace a few of the wasted years of my former life; that all the dear readers may know and appreciate God's wondrous works in connection with my salvation. God has been so merciful and good to me that it is with shame and sorrow I recall the past; but I am willing to endure both, if my feeble testimony can in any way glorify his holy name.

When quite a young girl (perhaps eleven years of age), a Methodist revival was being held in the little village where my parents lived, during which I became convicted and gave my heart to God. As these lines are penned, the occurrence rises vividly before me; for it was on that eventful night the wondrous power and glory of God stamped a hallowed impression upon my memory, which time could never efface, and which afterwards prevented me from becoming an infidel. When I was converted there did not seem to be any one among the M. E. professors present capable of instructing those who were at the altar; but Jesus, blessed Jesus met me there, and after penitently confessing my sins in a childish, innocent way, and being willing to sacrifice every thing to follow him, I grasped his precious promise, and received the blessed witness that my name was written in heaven.

Time wore away, but as I was totally ignorant of sanctification, and had received but few instructions regarding my duty to the dear Redeemer, before many months elapsed, the pleasures of the world turned my heart in rebellion away from God. Ere long I was married, and eight years of my life were afterwards spent amid the giddy whirl of fashion and society.

Infidel literature was continually strewn across my pathway, and much of my time was spent in reading "Tom Payne's Age of Reason;" Huxley's and Darwin's works; also D. M. Bennet's ungodly, appalling publications; in addition to many other infidel books and papers unnecessary to mention. Oh, the matchless love and mercy of Almighty God, to spare my unworthy life!

My husband, though noble, kind, affectionate and true, was an infidel, and accepted science and philosophy rather than the Bible; and being a man whom the great Creator had endowed with a superior intellect, many of his friends were willing to be guided by his anti-religious theories, with which I came in contact daily. I loved my husband as only a wife and mother can love, and as I was only seventeen years of age, while he was many years my senior, I always looked to him in childish confidence for guidance and protection; and no doubt would have been led to infidelity if it had not been for my former religious experience.

I could not doubt the existence of a Savior. With all the influences of infidelity that were brought to bear upon me, the memory of that hallowed night when God's mighty power flooded my soul, always seemed to rise like an image before me, and beat back the powers of darkest unbelief. I never could doubt the existence of a mighty God, after having felt his Holy Spirit within my soul; and so, through every conflict, I always steadfastly maintained the knowledge of a blessed Savior's existence.

But to return to the subject of my own life. For years I reveled in the gratification of every foolish whim, spending thousands of dollars for magnificent wearing apparel, and costly household articles of decoration. We were living in Allegheny City, Pa., a portion of the time, and my companions, though educated and refined, were gay butterflies of fashion like myself, flitting hither and thither to theatres, receptions, and all manner of worldly amusements. Every foolish luxury that wealth could afford, I partook of, and frequently walked upon the city streets clad in a small fortune of seal-skin, lace, silk, and diamonds, forgetful of the hungry mouths, and destitute homes of wretched families, whose thin, tattered mantles were insufficient to cover their nakedness from the cruel winter winds.

I did not stop to consider that one glittering gem upon my finger would purchase food and clothing for many wretched, groveling human beings, who came across my pathway daily, with wan, haggard faces and hollow eyes, begging alms. Oh God! why art thou so mindful of me, when so many years of my life were spent in devotion to worldly idols, and the time, talent, health, wealth and strength which thou didst give me, were spent in serving the adversary of my soul! " But time onward flows like a river vast," changing the course of our lives. With all the friends, wealth, vanity, and dazzling splendor of worldly allurements, my hungry soul was never satisfied—money could not buy the heavenly manna I craved for. Pride must fall. The all-seeing eye of

Almighty God beheld my pitiful and deplorable condition; he saw the gloom within my wretched soul, and in his faithfulness saw the necessity of afflicting me that I might learn to " lay up treasures in heaven."

The first blow of his chastening rod fell upon my rebellious heart a little more than three years ago. To me there was nothing more delightful in this world than to be seated around the family fireside with my husband and only child; but God had numbered my idols, and smote the family oak—whose branches had sheltered my boy and me from toil, care and want for so many years. On the 31st day of May, 1888, a team of horses ran away and plunged upon the helpless form of my husband, injuring him so severely that his entire body became instantly paralyzed, in which condition he lingered four long months in untold agony. Only his head and neck were alive, the balance of his body was apparently lifeless. One day during his terrible illness, while I was suffering indescribable mental anguish, these words were spoken by the Savior to my soul, "Whom the Lord loveth he chasteneth." Instead of falling upon my knees in humble submission to his holy will, I scoffed and jeered in the face of the Almighty and just God. I said it was not justice that a kind father and loving husband should be taken from me, when there were so many cruel and worthless drunkards in the world who abused their families. Verily, "My thoughts are not your thoughts, neither are your ways my ways, saith the Lord." Oh, the appalling rebellion, sin and woe that reigned within my cruel, wretched heart! Of all mortals I felt that I was most miserable. At times when my husband's sufferings were so severe, I would frantically leave the house, and wander through the fields, calling upon God desparingly. With prayers and tears I would look up to the blue arched heavens, and implore the Lamb of God to let my husband die, that I might not behold the scene any longer. On the 28th day of September, death came with its stern decree and summoned the soul of the one I loved so well, to eternity. But withal, God's hand had not yet completed the destruction of my earthly idols. Verily, "Thou shalt have no other gods before me." "I, the Lord thy God, am a jealous God." After the burial of my husband I discovered that I had become a physical wreck. I had always been so vain over my robust appearance, but God in his faithfulness had permitted my health to be taken from me, and I became emaciated, haggard and wan (another idol shattered that he afterwards might be glorified); and within a few days I received a telegram stating that my mother was seriously ill and not expected to live. I believe God called me to her bedside, that I might meet his ministering angel, Brother Warner, who pointed out to me the way of life; for when I arrived at my mother's home she was out of danger and rapidly recovering. Ofttimes it seemed I was doomed to come in contact with the children of God. They all were plainly dressed. Some of them were very poor, and lived in humble homes—but their time-worn clothing covered souls that were redeemed and made white by the blood of the Lamb. " By their fruits ye shall know them." And verily I have proved this to be true. The beauty —not of outward adornment, but of their daily lives —preached sermons to me which I could not escape from nor fail to behold. If I called upon the sick, God's ministering angels were there before me, with loving hearts and sun-browned, toil-worn hands, rendering both spiritual and temporal aid. Whenever or wherever I met with God's little ones the beauty of their works followed them. But how vastly different was my unhappy, worthless life! Money proved a curse to me. I spent it recklessly, without benefit to myself or those around me, and the fruit of my works was a bitter, remorseful conscience. So it seemed the blessed Savior's will that my silver and gold should take its departure through various losses as well as through my own extravagance. My heart was so proud and rebellious, God in his wisdom saw the great necessity of chastening my stubborn will

OF SOUL AND BODY. 213

into subjection through death, loss of health, property and friends. Oh praise his holy name forever and ever! In addition to the awful chastening I received I was much of the time under deep conviction. Wherever I went, a sweet low voice murmured to my soul, " I will guide thee with mine eye." I could not escape those thrilling words. They followed me through the long dreary hours of the night. When the world seemed to be asleep, and I would rise in my loneliness and desolation to weep, I could feel the all-searching eye of Almighty God penetrating the darkened chambers of my hungry soul. I was starving, famishing for something, and knew not what. For an interval of almost three years my condition remained unchanged. During this time I passed through indescribable mental anguish because of a law-suit which involved my husband's estate. Those of my friends or relatives whose duty it was to protect my child and me, left us alone in the world in our grief and desolation, to learn life's lesson among strangers. And we endured persecutions which God alone will reveal in final doom, but with all the awful chastenings I had received from the hand of the Lord, my heart was still rebellious, and again terrible bodily afflictions were permitted to come upon me, until at times my life was almost despaired of. It was during a severe attack of illness that I promised to yield to God's

Holy Spirit if he would spare my unworthy life, and his blessed hand raised me up that I might fulfill my promise.

Ten months ago during the month of February, I was stopping at my father's home, when Brother Dillon began a series of revival meetings in an adjoining building. It was only a few steps from our door to the saints' meeting-house. While sitting in my room I could hear the songs of Zion, and the prayers of the redeemed as they ascended to the throne of grace. For the first time in years I came to the full realization that it was the blood of Christ my hungry soul was yearning for. After struggling against conviction for so long, I attended an ordinance meeting, and there resolved to spend eternity with Christ. Many of the saints were present, and as I, the chief of sinners, knelt at the mercy seat, a chorus of hallelujahs poured forth in volumes to the throne of God. O praise his holy name forever! Amen and amen! I had never heard a prayer in my father's house, and as my father was present on that occasion, and witnessed the scene of his own flesh and blood struggling until nearly midnight against the powers of hell, his face seemed transformed into an image of marble. The dear ones labored with me until their strength seemed to be exhausted, but I did not meet God's requirements, and still remained a captive.

At last meeting was dismissed, and as my little boy and I wended our way homeward, a violent storm was raging, while the wind and rain beat upon us with relentless fury. Amid all this, when we could hardly see our way before us, the sweet childish face of my innocent boy was upturned to me in perfect confidence, and he said, "Dear Mamma, you are a saint now; I am going to trust you more than ever before; for I know you will always tell me the truth." Oh what a precious lesson those few words were!—to look to Jesus in that same childish confidence amid the awful tempest that was raging in my soul. The following day my peace was made with God through faith and repentance, after which I presented my body a "living sacrifice, holy, acceptable to God, which was my reasonable service." I consecrated my time, talent, friends, property, character and will, in connection with every earthly tie, all that I could think of and all that I could not think of. Every earthly joy which had formerly afforded me pleasure in a worldly way, all were placed on the altar Christ Jesus. Then and then only did his blessed word assure me that the altar sanctified the gift. O praise his holy name! All that I have and all that I am I owe to Christ, and to his blessed name give all the glory; and I know that he has not chastened me for pleasure, but of necessity that my soul might be saved from eternal doom. I not only accepted this wonderful Savior as the great Redeemer of my soul, but also as the divine healer of all physical ailments. Shortly after I was saved I became seriously ill, and was so weakened with pain and fever caused by La Grippe that it was difficult for me to raise my head from the pillow; but in accordance with his blessed word I called for the elders, who laid hands on me in Jesus' name. Instantly I was healed and arose from my bed. Praise his dear name forever and ever! At different times the dear Lord has raised me from beds of affliction when I was so weak and ill it seemed that I would die. Oh how can I praise my God enough! He has redeemed my unworthy soul, and gives me a pure heart. He has given me grace to stand beside my mother's coffin with heavenly resignation to his blessed will. He has enabled me to endure persecutions with perfect victory, which were sufficient to make me insane. He has removed all pride and worldly conformity from my heart as far as the East is from the West. He has by a bitter past experience pointed out to me the great necessity of lifting up my voice like a trumpet to cry against the vanity of this world, which in former years was dragging my own wretched soul to eternal ruin. He has enabled me to make wrongs right, and has filled my soul with peace, love and rest. One hour of

OF SOUL AND BODY. 217

sweet communion with my God I would not exchange for all the former years of my life of worldly pleasure. What is society but deception? what is vanity but a curse? What is wealth but a transitory comfort? which in most cases has a tendency to plunge souls into eternal ruin. Let us therefore be satisfied with such things as we have; for when time shall be no more, will the great Ruler of heaven and earth award everlasting life to those whose soft white hands, decked with glittering gems, have been idly folded on richly embroidered satin and damask all through the fleeting years of their worthless lives? Nay, verily the horny-handed reapers, who come from God's great harvest field, bringing the fruits of their labors with them, these are they whose voices shall blend in grand harmonious hallelujahs, when these words are spoken: "Well done, good and faithful servants," enter into the joy of thy Lord. Amen and amen.

Yours saved and sanctified.

BIRDIE E. FINK.

A WARNING AGAINST OPIUM.

About thirty years ago the dreadful disease of consumption came upon me, with an awful cough. All kinds of medicines that could be obtained were used, but in a few years it seemed that relief was a failure, and my case became a hopeless one. My body was a mass of disease, and wrecked with pain, insomuch that tongue cannot express the sufferings through which I passed. Strong tea and smoking tobacco were excessively used, and I was also advised to take opium. Not knowing the evil effects of it, I began using it, and soon the habit fastened upon me. If at any time I was deprived of opium it seemed as if a million red hot needles were piercing me, and I suffered the agonies of death until again supplied with the stuff to which I was enslaved.

After I was converted, in answer to prayer my health became some better for a time, but I continued the use of opium, not being fully awakened to the great evil of such a habit, and knowing my utter inability to give it up.

Before I was sanctified I had to consecrate to quit taking opium and risk my life entirely in God's hands, and when I had given up all things he sanctified my soul, and swept away the appetite. Two days afterward I had hands laid on me for my complete healing, after having been shown in the night that it was his will to heal me.

My long sickness had left me almost a skeleton, and my body was a mass of disease and corruption, steeped with the poison of opium and drugs. But the Lord spoke the words and I was healed. Then I became hungry and could eat almost any good wholesome food without injury. Immediately after the healing power came upon me a cleansing process began, and my system was relieved of all poisonous effects, and my body was left very weak. The brethren laid on hands and asked God to fill me with his Holy Spirit, and the power of God came upon me. I arose, leaped and shouted, and went to meeting and the Lord spoke through me in mighty power. Blessed be his name!

For one week after being healed I stayed with a sister in Christ and attended the meetings, and each day my husband and children would come with opium, but always finding me improving did not offer it to me. I cannot find words strong enough to warn people against the use of opium. A person can so easily become a slave to it, but when once enslaved nothing but the power of God will break its chains. The Lord keeps me wonderfully saved and healed.

Mrs. F. A. Abbott.

Bangor, Mich., *Aug. 5, 1891*.

DEVILS CAST OUT.

I wish to testify to the mighty power of God in delivering my soul from the power of Satan. I was born Dec. 2, 1867, near Jerry City, O., where I lived until about one year ago. My parents being saved I had religious teaching, and was saved at the age of

13 years. At the age of 16 years I went into the world to do for myself. Associating with the unsaved and going to places of worldly amusement, I soon lost the love of God and went back into sin, and fell into all the evil habits that are so common to the young men of to day, until I became a miserable sinful wretch. I shunned Christian society, disregarded the admonition of friends and parents, and rejected the word of God and the conviction of his Holy Spirit. This reckless course was pursued until about the 1st of October, 1889, when, one night just after going into my room, the Spirit of God spoke to me like a voice from heaven, saying, "How long will you continue in this condition?" I promised the Lord that if he would spare my life for two years then I would give my heart to him. But the voice said, "You must decide to night." I said, "Lord, I cannot start now." In an instant after this decision I saw a demon face approaching me. I tried to resist it, but could not help myself; the awful grinning face came straight to mine, then a fearful, clammy, choking sensation seized hold of me, and I could not get my breath. I saw that the devil had taken possession of my body. I ran out doors and knelt down by a tree and asked God to have mercy on me, and I would give my heart to him. I felt some better, but still there was something like a large lump in my breast,

OF SOUL AND BODY.

which at times would come up in my throat and choke me almost to death. I tried to live better, but could not. The devil led me captive to his will. Every night a spell of terrible fear would come upon me. My friends would sit up with me. The devil made me believe I had sinned against the Holy Ghost. I was in this condition until the 9th of Nov., 1889, when in one of these spells that voice that I had rejected came to me again, saying, "If you start to night you can be saved." Bless the Lord! I grasped the promise, sent for the elders of the church, and confessed to them my condition, and they laid hands on me in the name of the Lord and prayed for me, and the Lord cast out the evil spirits. I then repented of my sins, and God forgave them all. About two weeks after, I was sanctified; and am now living every day free from sin, and preaching to others this wonderful salvation.

Yours in him.

W. J. HENRY.

THE BLIND AND LAME SEE AND WALK.

I do thank Almighty God that he has so willed it that I can write with my own hand and tell of his mighty power to heal, save and keep me. Glory and praises to his blessed name! And I can truly say, Once I was lame, now I can walk; once I was blind, now I can see. I can say as did the woman of old, My faith has made me whole. One of His precious promises is, "If ye ask in faith believing, ye shall receive." I asked in faith, and I did receive. Glory to his name! And from the moment I was healed—two weeks ago to night—I have not had an ache or pain, neither do I get weary. I can work, and walk anywhere,—something I had not been able to do for two years.

I was severely injured by a fall, which resulted in epileptic fits, and was getting worse all the time. I was taken to my bed the 7th of January, and became so bad that I lost my mind and eyesight. The doctors said I would never get well. And I never would by human skill, but the great Physician, our Savior Jesus Christ, the healer of all diseases, saw fit in his kind providence to restore me to health and strength. "God moves in a mysterious way his wonders to perform."

I know if I live a hundred years and work for him, I can never repay him for his goodness and mercy to unworthy me. My daily prayer is that I may live a pure, humble, devoted Christian life, and tell others of his power to heal the body as well as the soul. If we ask in faith believing, the prayer of the righteous availeth much.

I cannot find words to express what is in my heart

what I saw and the way I felt when I was healed. I can only say it was direct answer from God to my prayer of faith. I must close by saying, The half has not been told. I ask an interest in your prayers that I may be kept humble and faithful unto the end, and that I may be a bright and shining light for him who did so much for me.

Yours in Christ.

MINNIE CHAPMAN.

Dayton, Ohio, *Feb. 27, 1892.*

BROKEN BONE HEALED.

I rejoice to know that I am saved just now, and can say as the apostle Paul said, "For we know that if our earthly house of this tabernacle were dissolved, we have a building of God, a house not made with hands, eternal in the heavens."—2 Cor. 5: 1. "For the Lord is my light and my salvation; whom shall I fear? the Lord is the strength of my life; of whom shall I be afraid?"—Psa. 27: 1. I praise the Lord for the salvation of my soul, and for the healing of my body. I was kicked by a cow and my limb was broken. We sent not for an earthly physician, but for the elders of the church, as the Word teaches, and by prayer and laying on of hands the pain was all taken away, and I began to amend; and next day I walked about with a crutch, bearing some weight on my broken limb. This caused quite a stir among the people, and the devil got very mad, and caused a falsehood to be published in several newspapers, which the people read, and came for miles to see what great harm had come to me by trusting the Lord: but, praise the Lord! to their astonishment they found it as the people did in the case of the viper fastening to Paul's hand. Acts 28: 6. No harm came to me; for God both set the bone and healed my limb, without even a bandage, for which I give Him all the glory.

Your sister in the body of Christ.

MATILDA M. BRAGG.

Sweetser, Ind., *April 1, 1890.*

AN ANOINTED HANDKERCHIEF APPLIED.

I feel it a great privilege to add my testimony with that of others, in the book on Divine Healing. I have been most wonderfully led of the Holy Spirit, out into this blessed evening light, before knowing of such a chosen people of God.

After hearing of them, I was sick unto death with "La Grippe." Doctors helped some but finally failed, and said that my system was full of 'Grippe' poison. My extremity was God's opportunity. I wanted an evidence from God that this people were right, but I did not think of it when I wrote and asked Brother Byrum to pray for my healing. I

OF SOUL AND BODY. 225

asked to be anointed by faith, not even thinking of St. Paul's sending out handkerchiefs and aprons from his body. I was greatly surprised upon receiving the anointed handkerchief from our brother, and felt a power of God upon me from it when I took it in my hands. At the hour set apart for prayer for me, I applied the handkerchief, *nothing doubting*. In three days after there was a special manifestation of divine power, and in five days I found myself free from all "Grippe" poison. In a short time I was especially led of God to a camp-meeting, and there the elders laid on hands for the full return of my strength. It came at once, and I never knew such health and strength in my younger days as I have had since. Praise God forever! After my return from camp-meeting, Sister Hattie Marsh was brought low upon a sick bed, from the effects of "La Grippe," and injuries received at child-birth, which had become chronic, the inflammation being great. Her physician said there was no more help for her. I was with her most of the time for a week. Her case was a sad one—a mother of small children, and almost in despair, having no faith for herself; saying that it was for such as myself but not for her to be healed, as she was not good enough. God over-ruled such ideas, and I wrote for prayer for her, and the anointing. On the Sabbath day, when prayers were offered for her, she was in great confusion and greatly tempted, but very quiet. We prayed at the hour set apart, and then waited upon God quietly for several hours. Again we prayed, and applied the anointed handkerchief over the diseased parts. Her confusion left her, her faith took hold of God her sins were forgiven, and she was healed. She arose from her bed and went about the house with her face lighted up with a heavenly smile which we had never seen upon it before, and which does not become less.

Dear suffering ones, whoever and wherever you are, you that are living without a hope of ever being any better, oh! let us entreat you and prevail with you, to put on courage, and look to Jesus. The virtue that was in Christ to heal the sick eighteen hundred years ago, has lost none of its power, but is the same to day.

Mrs. Melissa Lane.

Binghamton, N. Y.

THE CHASTENING ROD.

Believing that it would be to the glory of God, I will write a little of my experience, showing how terribly God laid his chastening hand upon me; and how wonderfully and miraculously he delivered me when engulfed in the deepest sorrow and anguish of mind known to man on earth.

While living in a cold profession, being a member of the U B. sect, although counted one of the faithful ones, I was constantly reminded (as every one who is deficient will be) that I was not doing all that I could do to please my Master. In the spring of 1880 God's chastening hand was laid heavily upon me. Sleep was taken away from me, and for about four and one-half months I do not think that I slept twelve hours; although I usually limit the time to twenty-four hours, to be sure that I make no misstatement. This was obtained by sleeping medicine, of which I would take a sufficient amount to put a well man to sleep so that I think he would never wake. Sometimes I would get a few minute's sleep, if sleep it might be called. But often even this failed to put me to sleep. During this time terrible things were revealed to me concerning my eternal welfare, of which I will only give a part, fearing that I shall be too lengthy. I was cast into hell, whether in the body or out of the body I cannot tell; but it seemed to me in the body. First a voice said to me, "This is the punishment you shall receive for the way you have lived." And I was cast into the lake that burneth with fire and brimstone, only for a few seconds. First I sank under, then came up and floated on top, and I can testify to the awful pains and pangs of hell as being indescribable. It seemed to be more than I could endure and live. A few days after this I had a vision. I saw, while awake, three angels high in the heavens float out in their beautiful long robes. And one opened a book and began to read: Then shall the kingdom of heaven be likened unto ten virgins, which took their lamps and went forth to meet the bridegroom; five of them were wise, and five were foolish. And a voice said to me, You are one of the foolish virgins; and that I had no oil in my lamp. During all my affliction I was just as rational as I have ever been; and prayed to God day and night that I might be delivered. But God continually deepened my sorrows by showing me that in my condition I was eternally lost. At the close of this chastisement I saw a beautiful fiery scroll in the heavens, after which I was again set free. Life now seemed sweeter than ever before. Old things became new. While once I read the Word of God because I felt it my duty, now I love it and my Savior above all things. I now felt a call to go into the work for the Lord. But I refused. The Spirit pressed upon me so heavily, and desiring some other evidence, I would take my testament in my hand and say to the Lord, If you want me in the work, let it open to such a place; and it would open

OF SOUL AND BODY.

to that place. Not willing to take this as an evidence, I would name another place, and ask again, and it would open to that place. Then I would say that it just happened so. Often I would ask, and the Lord would answer in this way. Then I would say, Lord, if you want me in the work, speak it plainly to me and I will go. For nearly ten years I grieved the Lord in this way until he again laid his chastening hand upon me. Sleep was again taken away from me, and for nearly six months no one could comprehend without a similar experience how terrible the agonies which I passed through. One hour seemed as long as three. Many times in various ways I had planned to take my own life. But the Lord always prevented. The Lord showed me plainly that if I had been patient he would not have chastened me so severely. I would often say that if I knew that I would ever be delivered, then I could be patient. But after pleading so long with God for mercy and deliverance, and promising to obey him and be obedient in all things, and yet finding no release, I would grow impatient and try to convince the Lord that he was unjust to still continue this terrible affliction upon me.

During this last chastisement, while awake, a voice from above spoke plainly to me, saying, By the grace of God you may live always. There is a work for you to do. I give to you the keys of the kingdom of heaven, and whatsoever you shall bind on earth shall be bound in heaven, and whatsoever you shall loose on earth shall be loosed in heaven.

Shortly after this the subject of a message which God has given me to put before the world, was given to me; viz., That popular ministers of the Gospel are leading more souls to eternal despair than all other institutions of evil combined: and to prove it by the Word of God.

Yours in Christ.

W. S. BANGS.

Alma, Mich.

A FRIEND IN AFFLICTION.

We will remember in asking God to heal our bodies that he says, "Who forgiveth all thine iniquities; who healeth all thy diseases." It was also good for me to be afflicted that I might learn the statutes of the Lord.

In 1886 the Lord pardoned my sins and made me to rejoice in his love. But, like a great many others, I joined the Methodist sect; but to be sure, if we walk in the light, as he is in the light, the blood will cleanse us from all sin. The Lord did not permit me to lose my experience until I received the light on coming out of Babylon, and rejected it. God convicted me

OF SOUL AND BODY. 231

for baptism; having been sprinkled in the M. E. sect, he wonderfully convinced me that he had not accepted sprinkling as baptism for me. I went on in this condition about six months, very miserable indeed, realizing the wrath of God upon me. And God permitted a dreadful affliction to come upon me, which I thought at the time would take my life, and I knew that if I died in that condition I would be lost. "The pains of hell gat hold upon me; the sorrows of death compassed me about. I cried unto the Lord, and he heard me, and delivered me out of my distresses," and once more pardoned my sins. I had all the medical aid that I needed for nearly three months, which seemed to avail but little. Sometimes I would receive temporary relief therefrom, but no permanent cure was effected. But when I did every thing that God required of me,—that was, to come out of Babylon, and promise God that I would be baptized by immersion in the name of Jesus,—he filled my soul with his glory and healed my body. Praise the Lord forever for his wonderful works to the children of men! It was on Wednesday when the Lord healed me, and I was baptized the Sunday following. Truly God witnessed my baptism by his Holy Spirit, and I never enjoyed anything more in my life.

On Wednesday after I was baptized I had a great trial of my faith. The devil brought back all the symptoms of the disease, and tried very hard to make me doubt that the Lord had healed me; but praise our God, who always causeth us to triumph, that he did give me victory! "For this is the victory that overcometh the world, even our faith." And again he says: "Cast not away therefore your confidence, which hath great recompense of reward. Praise God for the reward of faith! The Lord did all for me that I was able to trust him for. Although for about six months I could not do very much hard work, not knowing how to trust the Lord for much as well as little; but since that time, which is now over three years, the Lord has wonderfully strengthened me, and has enabled me to do as much work as most any one else, for which I do give God all the glory. O how much I realize the 2d verse of the 30th Psalm as being my experience, which reads as follows: "O Lord my God, I cried unto thee, and thou hast healed me!" And also Jas. 4: 10.—"Humble yourselves in the sight of the Lord, and he will lift you up." I have always found him a friend in time of affliction.

Your sister, sanctified and healed by the power of God.

MARY E. LAMBERT.

Givens, Tenn.

OF SOUL AND BODY.

CRUTCHES THROWN AWAY.

I feel it to the glory of God, and for the benefit of those who are afflicted, that I testify to the wonderful healing power of God. All my life since I was two and one-half years old I have been a cripple, afflicted with hip disease, and all I was able to walk at all, I had to use a crutch and cane, till I was nineteen years old. But the first four years of that time I was not able to help myself out of bed, or walk a step. I suffered pain beyond description.

For about thirteen years my parents employed the best physicians they could find, and tried every means to restore the use of that hip. But in spite of all they could do the hip was drawn out of joint, and grew out of place. (It is now nearly six inches shorter than the other.) After they found the leg could not be cured, and made whole like the other they tried every means to remove the pain, but all to no avail. The doctors gave it up. They said I must suffer on and in a few years die with the pain. I gave up all medicines in despair, never expecting to see a day free from pain. About three years after giving up medical treatment, I heard the true gospel preached, and on the twenty-third of January, 1883, I became acquainted with God, and realized the pardon of my sins. I heard some testify to God's healing power, so I immediately began to search the scriptures to see if these things were so. I found he New Testament full of such cases wrought in olden times; then the question came, can such things be done now? The Bible before me answered: "God is the same yesterday, to day and forever." But do we have any right to pray for such things now? My Bible answered: "Is any among you afflicted, let him pray."—Jas. 5: 13. But does this really mean poor unworthy me? "Every one that asketh receiveth."—Matt. 7: 8.

On what condition? "Whatsoever we ask we receive of him, because we keep his commandments, and do those things that are pleasing in his sight." —1 John 3: 22. "And all things whatsoever ye shall ask in prayer, *believing, ye shall receive*."—Matt.21: 22. That was enough for me; I must ask; I must keep his commandments; I must do those things that are pleasing in his sight; I must believe his promises to be sure, then I should receive. In this way I looked to God with confidence (1 John 5: 14, 15) and asked for the pain to be removed from my hip. Instantly it was done. All the pain left while I was yet praying alone with God. It is now over eight years since God removed the pain, and I have never had a moment's pain in my hip since. This strengthened my faith to ask for more. In a few days I began to believe God could help me to walk without my crutch, so I asked the

Lord about it, and the small voice whispered, "Jesus is all the crutch you need; trust in him." I immediately threw my crutches aside and have never felt the need of them since. The instant I began to walk by faith, trusting God for strength, I felt strength come, and I have felt no weakness in that hip since.

I give God all the praise, for it was all done in answer to prayer, and was received while I was yet praying, and without the aid of medical treatment.

Yours in Christ.

J. A. SPAULDING.

413 Jane St., Kalamazoo, Mich., *July 15, 1891.*

HEALING OF CANCER AND CONSUMPTION.

"He that dwelleth in the secret place of the Most High shall abide under the shadow of the Almighty. I will say of the Lord, He is my refuge and my fortress: my God; in him will I trust. Surely he shall deliver thee from the snare of the fowler, and from the noisome pestilence. He shall cover thee with his feathers, and under his wings shalt thou trust: his truth shall be thy shield and buckler." —Psalms 91: 1-4.

In the fall of 1886 I was healed of cancer and consumption by the power of God, through the laying on of an anointed handkerchief, as taught in Acts

19: 12. For about six years I suffered with consumption, and with cancer for three years.

We traveled from place to place in search of the climate that would cure consumption. I would get relief for a short time, but as soon as I became acclimated my health would decline, and hemorrhages return. I felt that my stay on earth with my two little children would be very short. I had been in the doctor's care, used Scott's Emulsion of Cod Liver Oil, and drank blood as long as my stomach could retain it.

It was a desperate fight for life. Had it not been for my desire to raise my children, I should have been glad to have been at rest. I was so weak that to try to sing, or to sweep one room would bring on a slight hemorrhage.

O I do praise God for deliverance from this terrible suffering. I have been healed nearly five years, and am enjoying the best of health, and a salvation that saves to the uttermost. Praise God for a religion that loses sight of all creeds and doctrines of men!

Our daughter Lulu's healing was a wonderful miracle, and teaches us how God honors the faith of children. She suffered from a cancer in her face, and whenever it was troublesome, one in her stomach acted in sympathy with it. She suffered intense pain when she ate certain kinds of food, but there were times that her stomach would not retain any solid food. Cancer doctors gave me no encouragement. The final attack lasted two weeks. The first week she partook of a little solid food, but the second week, if she ate the least particle of food, her suffering was so great that I could hardly stay in the room. O how I plead with God to spare her life, that it should be entirely devoted to his work. She never knew from what disease she was suffering, until one day she asked me what caused the pain in her stomach. I hesitated a few moments, as I did not want to frighten her by telling the cause. The thought then came to me that if God sent a disease that we could not control, I should not let her go out of the world ignorant of the cause of the suffering. At that time I did not know that the devil was the author of disease. I told her the cause of her sickness; also that I was praying for her and that we would do all in our power for her. She replied that if God wanted her to suffer from a cancer in her stomach, she was willing. She left the room to pray, and came back with a bright, happy look on her face, and asked for something to eat. I must confess that her faith was stronger than mine. I prepared a cup of cracker soup, which she ate, and all honor to our Physician who healeth all our diseases; she was healed from that moment, and has never felt a symptom of the disease since.

Your sister in Christ.

ANNA E. ALBRIGHT.

San Diego, Cal., *Nov. 26, 1891.*

THE LORD IS MY PHYSICIAN.

Nearly two years ago I was taken with a bad diarrhœa and piles, insomuch that I was unable to work. I could receive no benefit from doctors or any one else. I staid two weeks with a doctor, who performed a surgical operation, but it did no good. Finally I found that the more medicine that was used, the worse I became, and soon came to the conclusion if ever a cure was effected God would have to do it.

I had read of faith cures, and heard of persons being healed by faith, and knew that the Word of God taught it, but knew of no one who claimed the power of healing by faith, except a "science cure" woman. But when told how she did the work, I concluded that I did not want to mortgage my soul to the devil for health. I began to pray for the Lord to send some one who had faith, that I might be healed. I gave up the use of medicine, and said I would take no more; and thought that if the Lord was going to heal me, no more medicine was needed.

I believe this is the consecration every one must make if they would be healed of the Lord. God soon sent a brother who preached the Gospel in its purity, but my faith was not strong enough to believe for healing. I read in the GOSPEL TRUMPET— a holiness journal published at Grand Junction, Mich., —about how God had worked through certain brethren on the line of faith healing. I attended a campmeeting in Gratiot County, Mich., and while there called for the elders, and was anointed with oil in the name of the Lord, and was healed, for which I give God all the praise and glory.

Last winter I had a very severe attack of La Grippe, but some brethren came and I applied for healing, and the Lord instantly healed me. Since then I was taken sick with the same disease, and knew of no saints near enough to call to my assistance; so I called upon the Lord and he heard me, and healed me. Blessed be his name!

SHERMAN L. CATLIN.

Muskegon, Mich., *July 15, 1891.*

A WONDERFUL ANSWER TO PRAYER.

I desire to honor God by telling what he has done for me. A short time ago I was greatly afflicted with an abscess on my side, which caused such intense pain and suffering that I was near death's door. It became so bad that I could not move my arm. For three weeks I suffered in this way, taking morphine to kill the pain; but as soon as the effect of the morphine would leave, the pain would return as bad as ever. The doctor lanced it three times, and refused to do it any more. During this time I had failed to call upon God to heal me, until one night the Lord showed me in a dream that it was my privilege to be healed; so I sent for some of God's children to come and pray for me, but my faith did not seem to take hold of God for the healing. Shortly afterward I sent for some more of the brethren, who came and anointed me with oil and laid on hands, and the pain immediately left, and I was enabled to use my arm; but that night the pain seemed to come back worse than ever, and I thought the Lord was going to take me home to live in his heavenly kingdom: so I called my family to my bedside and kissed them and bade them good bye, and told them I was going to die. But my wife said, "No, the Lord will heal you," and that seemed to give me courage, and the Lord impressed me more than ever that I could be healed. So I sent at once to the TRUMPET office for Bro. Warner and Bro. Byrum to pray for me, and they arose from their beds—as it was about midnight—and asked God to heal me. And before my boy returned I was healed. The pain left instantly. The Lord did the lancing and did a complete work of it, and ever since that time I have been entirely free from pain. I am healed by the power of God. Blessed be his name! To him I give all the glory.

I can recommend the Lord as a great physician, who forgiveth all our iniquities; who healeth all our diseases.—Psa. 103: 3. I am saved and sanctified, washed and redeemed through the blood of Jesus.

C. MAJOR.

Grand Junction, Mich., *Feb. 27, 1890.*

A CHANGE OF PHYSICIANS.

Some years ago a wonderful case of healing was wrought in my family in answer to the prayer of faith.

My child, who is now a fine, healthy boy of fourteen years, was then a poor little child of five summers, and at the time spoken of seemed to be at the point of death. My husband wanted to change physicians, and so did I, but the difference between us was, he wanted another one of the earthly sort, while I wanted to trust the Great Physician, Jesus Christ. He yielded to my request, but left me alone with my child and my God. The doctor's medicine was all gone, and the thought came to me that he will be dead before a doctor can get here. These words came to my mind: " Man's extremity is God's opportunity;" next, "The prayer of faith shall save the sick." I questioned myself thus: 1st, Do you believe that God can heal that child? My answer was, "Yes, he made him." 2d, If it is God's will to take him, can you submit? I answered, "Thy will be done, O God.', Then came the sweet assurance that the work would be done; and as I laid a cloth wet with cold water upon his face, my faith took hold of the promise, and the work was done that instant. Praise God forever and ever!

EMMA I. COSTON.

Muskegon, Mich.

CONFIRMING TESTIMONY.

The author has requested us to add our testimony of some things we have witnessed of the healing power of God. To the glory of Him who worketh all things in the members of his redeemed church, we will speak of a few instances out of the hundreds, and could truthfully say thousands, of healing miracles that we have beheld in the last fifteen years.

Out of the gratitude of my heart I would first acknowledge the good hand of God that has been upon myself. I had long been afflicted with a very bad cough, and was pronounced a consumptive over twenty-five years ago, when I yielded to the solemn call of God to preach his Gospel. He then promised to heal and sustain me, and he has remembered his covenant unto his unworthy servant in a marvelous manner. He has been my strength in all my labors, and has many times instantaneously and wondrously healed me of various afflictions. Blessed be his name forever!

I was a witness to the great miracle performed upon Sister Lodema Kaser, reported in this work. She was carried into the house as helpless as a dead person and nearly as unconscious. After the Lord healed her internal injuries, and removed the dreadful chill that had seized upon her almost lifeless body, she found her arm crushed and in great pain. A sister undertook an examination, but the pain was so great she could scarcely bear to have her arm moved or the wound touched. So we desisted, saying, "The Lord knows all about it and that is enough." We placed our hands on the arm as lightly as possible, and called upon the Lord to heal it. Instantly his Spirit witnessed that it was done, and she held up her arm and praised the Lord. Presently her restored arm embraced Sister Cole, after which she arose every whit whole.

A few days later Sister Kaser having excessively used her arm in work, the lately knit parts gave way and she felt the broken bones grate together. This circumstance enabled her to know more surely that her bones had been broken, and that God had indeed instantly knit and healed them. Continuing to trust God, and more carefully favoring that arm for a few days, it was all sound. Not long after, Dr. Bryant, of Galesburg, Kan., examined her arm, and informed her that it gave clear evidence of having been broken.

So it is evident that the same God who was skillful enough to create Eve out of a rib, also understands how to set and quickly restore broken bones, as well as heal all manner of diseases; and can be safely trusted under all circumstances.

One morning early, while our company were at Bro. Ahijah Bardens, near Walkerton, Ind., Brother Wolfenberger, having heard of our arrival, came after us to pray for the restoration of their sick boy, Perry. After breakfast Bro. Barden took us all to the place, and we found a very sick child indeed. A council of physicians the day before had pronounced it a very dangerous case of spinal fever. Shortly after we entered the house the attending physician came in, who was also a preacher. While he was making his examinations, dealing out his drugs, and giving directions for the doses to be imposed upon the poor little sufferer every hour and half hour, we were all communing with our God, and his glorious Spirit assured us the Lord would heal the boy. Fi

OF SOUL AND BODY.

nally the doctor remarked, "Perhaps my treatment interferes with other arrangements." The Spirit of God was wonderfully upon us, and moved us to speak as follows: "This family has called us here to pray for the healing of this child, and we believe God will do the work. But he must have the case entirely in his hands; for he does not practice in conjunction with the medical systems of men. And now it is for these parents to say whether they wish your treatment continued, or whether they will let the Lord take the case." Sister Wolfenberger immediately remarked, "We will give him into the hands of the Lord." And God instantly blessed her soul. We spoke in the Spirit, saying, "God is present to heal the child." The preacher-doctor ironically replied, "Then I'll stay and see it done." But ere we had time to frame a reply the Spirit of God spoke through our lips, "Perhaps God does not want you present. In olden times unbelievers were put out when the sick were to be healed, and the dead raised." The man had been opposing the work of God's holiness in the place, and these words stung him to the heart, to think that he, a preacher, was not a fit man to be present where God was to show his power. "So," said he, "you say I must leave, must I?" "No sir, I do not say so. God can do his work whether you are present or absent. But this you know very well, you have no fellowship with us; no faith in God for the healing of the sick and consequently, your presence is no benefit." He sat in silence, and confident that the mighty power of God would drive him out, we hesitated. Perhaps wishing to make capital of our ordering him out, he again said, "Then you say I must leave?" To which we replied, "No sir, I do not say you must leave, but God will have his own way." Praise God! he immediately took his departure.

The little sufferer was then anointed, and with difficulty we laid our hands upon him, as he was rolling about, extremely sick, and burning with fever. After prayer, by faith in God we pronounced him healed. Immediately his eyes opened, the fever left, and the skin became moist. As the affectionate family thronged his bed with tears of gratitude to God, Perry said to his sister, "Bring me a cookie." A large cookie was brought and eaten with much relish. "Bring me another cookie, and some meat," his keen appetite requested. They were brought and eaten as by a hungry laborer. He had taken scarcely any food for four days. In a few moments he was out of bed, sound and well, and continued so

While the father was gone after us, their daughter, who had been called home the night before by telegram, thought since they were going to apply to

OF SOUL AND BODY. 247

Jesus for the healing of her brother, she would honor him by giving her heart to the Lord. So she withdrew to a room and sought the Lord, and found peace to her soul. After witnessing the wonderful miracle, the hired girl also knelt down and called on God for mercy, and found peace in believing. And there was great joy in that house.

The wife of Bro. Elihu Bragg, a few miles from Sweetser, Grant county, Ind., had been near death's door for twelve days. We arrived in the neighborhood on Friday. The same evening a brother called and prayed with her, when she received a slight touch of the hand of God, and somewhat revived. Up to that time she had lain helpless for some days, and scarcely noticed anything around her. On Saturday we all met there. To quicken her faith, some scriptures were read, and some testimonies of healing were given. Finally the doctor who had called about the time we arrived, arose, and with tears remarked that he had once been converted. "But," says he, "I now see from your testimonies I should have gone on to a deeper experience. I also believe in the power of God to heal the sick, and I believe God will heal this woman to day." The mighty presence and power of God moved this testimony from his lips, to let us know that the doctor was not in the way of God's work. For that class are usually very skeptical in regard to God healing people, and some are even jealous of his work.

We drew the bed from the wall, and surrounded it upon our knees. After prayer, anointing, and the laying on of hands, God instantly raised up the poor woman. She sat up and praised God. Called for her clothes, dressed, and walked the floor praising the Lord. Some neighbors—sectarians—being present, pronounced it excitement, and predicted that she would be in her grave in three days. But, blessed be the name of the Lord! she continued well, and on Monday came three miles to the meeting, coming into the house leaping and shouting; and has ever since enjoyed better health than for years.

These cases we give as samples of the work we frequently behold wrought by the hand of our gracious and mighty Physician. Stiff arms have been instantly restored and raised up, with praises to God. Blind eyes have been opened, deaf ears unstopped. The lame have been made to cast away their crutches and canes, and walk and leap for joy. And about all kinds of diseases healed by the power of God, and in the almighty name of Jesus. To whom be all the praise and glory, world without end. Amen.   D. S. WARNER.

www.ingramcontent.com/pod-product-compliance
Lightning Source LLC
Chambersburg PA
CBHW020803230426
43666CB00007B/828